Awaken Your Wild You

Lissa Corra

Awaken Your Wild You

Lissa Corra
Copyright 2021

www.lissacorra.com

www.whitefernpublishing.com

Isbn 9798731575348

Dedicated with love always to

Margaret McPhee & Eliza Jane (Ella) Spowart

Awaken Your Wild You

Contents

Introduction   9

Thread 1   ***Sovereign***
- 1   What is Sovereignty?   17
- 2   Know Yourself   27
- 3   Values & Boundaries   33
- 4   Remember Reconnect Reclaim   43

Thread 2   ***Cycles***
- 5   Calendars ~ Seasons ~ Wheel of the Year   53
- 6   Lunar   80
- 7   Menstrual   90
- 8   Life   107
- 9   Remember Reconnect Reclaim   147

Thread 3   ***SHE***
- 10   Divine Feminine   157
- 11   Modern Spirituality   165
- 12   Connection   177
- 13   Remember Reconnect Reclaim   191

Thread 4   ***Circles***
- 14   When We Gathered   199
- 15   Why We Gather   205
- 16   How We Gather   213
- 17   Remember Reconnect Reclaim   223

Thread 5   ***Sacred***
- 18   Sacred Soul Sustenance   233
- 19   Rituals & Practices   247
- 20   Remember Reconnect Reclaim   259

Conclusion	267
Acknowledgements	271
About the Author	273

Divine Love Power

Lissa Corra

*Be yourself
in all your glory.
This is your life.
This is your story.*

~ Lissa Corra ~

Introduction

Deep in REM sleep your inner Wild is dreaming of the new dawn; untamed, sovereign and free. Free to be honest and raw, authentic without shame or fear, not clipped by conditioning. This sleep has been long, going back through the generations from you to your mother, your grandmother, right along the red thread that connects heart and womb back through time, through the burning times, the crusades to the rise of patriarchy and the Abrahamic religions with their one masculine God, to the first ancestors. She remembers when she was revered and respected for her wisdom and knowing, her connection with the Great Mother, the power of her blood and the community of sisters. She is dreaming of being allowed to be and is growing evermore restless. She is no longer held in that state of deep comfortable sleep. Her body temperature is rising and her heart beat is quickening. She is stirring.
Wakey wakey, rise and shine!

Are you asleep, coming to, awake? Not you as you are, but your inner you, your inner Wild.

This is your invitation to seek her out, go within to meet her, understand her and awaken to the fullness and completeness of you. Take the time to get curious and unravel everything you know, believe, value and trust; where did you learn these things, how did you come to understand them, do they still fit with who you are now or who you are becoming? Break it all down. Analyse it. Question it. **Be discerning.**

Explore the path and enjoy the journey. Our personal path and journey in life is as individual as we are. Walk it to see where it takes you and what you will discover on the way. Nobody does you like you do. Your voice has its own unique tone and strikes its own chord, let it be heard. I firmly believe that one size will never ever fit all and nor is it designed to, therefore, your experiences and journey will absolutely be different from mine and from what I share between these pages.

Get comfortable with being uncomfortable. When you've stepped so far out of your comfort zone that it becomes a mere dot, you will find out who you are and what you're capable of. Hello anxiety and fear, self discovery and growth as you face truths that may hurt your feelings, offend people that don't honour or respect your boundaries, and reject beliefs you have grown up with but never really thought about, until now. Have you outgrown your life style? Do you crave more of that which lights you up and less of that which depletes you? Get ready to feel nervous and excited to honour your truest self. On the days when you're feeling not enough or too much, when you need to reinforce (or establish) your boundaries, remember, you have the power, you are the power. You are the Creatrix of your own life and Mistress of your own magic; trust it (trust yourself) and use it.

You won't find your answers online or in a book, even this book, but from opening your mind, heart and intuition; awakening your inner Wild. Everything you are and have is already within you; the answers you seek, the divine, your power, your past, your present and your future. Question everything and every source and learn to judge for *yourself* what feels right or makes sense and discard the rest. What that will look like will differ for each and every one of us on this earth. As it should. Between these pages you are encouraged to delve into your own unique herstories and heritage, to understand and know the magic, power and wisdom that resides in your blood, bones and soul. Recognise, reclaim and rejoice in your rites of passage, your connection to the earth and to your ancestors. Remember, rediscover and unlearn who you are.

There is a need, right now, a primal desire, to live authentically in our truth. For when we do, we ignite the spark in each other and the collective awakens too. There is an untapped wellspring of support just waiting for permission to flow to enable the (re)creation of community and sisterhood, gathering together, rising together to connect with and encourage one another, rather than competing against one another.

Using this book to reawaken your Wild requires you to walk your own path and navigate your own journey according to your own compass, values and personal truths. I am giving you a framework and some tools to assist and guide you but I am not your teacher or guru. I can bring new ideas or points of view, but the work is yours. Explore it, participate, feel into it and trust the process. No-one else can do it for you, no one can live your life or tell your story for you. Living, breathing and embodying this life will allow you to fully experience it in all its glory; the highs and the lows, awakened and alive. Always evolving, shedding and starting over.

Are you wondering if this book is for you? Are you wondering what the point of the awakening is? Is it just another layer to aspire to, another role to play? I invite you to ask yourself how much has your integrity, your authenticity or your privacy been comprised on during this lifetime? You are here, book in hand, because your Wild is ready to awaken; she is stirring within, awaiting her release. Breach those boundaries and shackles of conformity and expectation. The only permission you need is your own. Belief in yourself is where the magic lives. Do you believe in you?

So, how do you awaken your wild you? Pause just for one second and first consider what it actually means to *you*, what does it look it? It will most likely look different for each woman reading this book today. It could be reconnecting with and owning your inner Witch, Bitch, Mary Magdalene, Crone, Maiden, Innocence, or Spiritual Way-shower. It could be simply showing up and being happy, content and comfortable with who you are today in this moment. It may look like reclaiming your voice, your womb, your body. It may look like reclaiming your fierce power or your quiet intuition. It could be releasing shame about who you are or what you've done or experienced in the past. It could be releasing regrets, expectation, conditioning, or old beliefs and familial traditions. It could be and will be anything and exactly what you want it and need it to be. And now back to the how; you will work and weave the threads of the wild tapestry of life. The threads of *Sovereign, Cycles, SHE, Circles* and *Sacred* are strong independent fibres but together are a potent blend of integrity, freedom and connection. This is Herstory in action. This doesn't need to be a grand gesture; changing a mindset is a start to making future herstory your story.

The order in which you weave your working is entirely up to you; create your own masterpiece. The threads and the chapters may be read in order or as you are called to do, as they all overlap and interweave though the course of time and each other. At the end of each thread there is a guided meditation to explore, questions to ask yourself and practical exercises for you to try. I do suggest having a journal to hand to record your thoughts, feelings, experiences and actions as you go, a record of your awakening Wild and allowing the Women's Mysteries to once again unfold, flourish and thrive.

Are you ready to awaken and meet your inner Wild or have you met her and are enjoying the dance through life? Are you ready to embark on this exploration as we spiral into the mists of your reawakening?

Awaken Your Wild You

THREAD ONE

SOVEREIGN

Your life
Your story
Your rules
Your plot twists
Your decisions
Your boundaries
Yours!

~ Lissa Corra ~

1

What is Sovereignty?

Wild is Sovereign.
Sovereign is Wild.
~ Lissa Corra ~

Sovereignty. Are you familiar with the word or its meaning? According the Collins English Dictionary, the definition of sovereign is:

- A **sovereign** *state or country is independent and not under the authority of any other country.*
- **Sovereign** *is used to describe the person or institution that has the highest power in a country.*

However we are not talking about a country or institution here, we are talking about ourselves.

Sovereignty is self-governance.

Sovereignty is freedom to make our own decisions with absolute and autonomous power for ourselves. It says :

"I have the power, I am the power to be and do as I choose."

Uncovering what it means to rewild, reclaim, remember, rise and stand sovereign in our own skin, in our purpose, truth and power starts with knowing what sovereignty means on a personal level.

Why is that important? When we honour our sovereignty we are the ones in control of our own actions, we can hold ourselves to account, discern what is right, make judgements and decisions that reflect our values, we know our own boundaries and know when they are being crossed, and whether we allow it or not. It puts our lives and destinies in our own hands. Sovereignty does not require permission from others to be who we are. It refuses to allow us to be cowed or to keep ourselves small or quiet lest we dare to dream or offend those to whom it would not be advantageous, including society in general. Yes there is a wild energy to sovereignty, but surely that is a good thing rather than one to fear and suppress?

Sovereignty is your super power.

What is so wrong with or scary about showing up as a whole human being rather than a copy of what has been decreed by society or the patriarchy or our parents or the church (or any other indoctrinated group think)? Are we really that collegiate when it comes to expressing and living our true essence?

In the "free world" we each have the right to sovereignty as free citizens, but how many of us are actually free and living our birth right as a sovereign being? We are taught from a very young age that we are to be nice, well behaved, good girls and that our elders know better (because when we are young, more often than not they do and that keeps us safe). That teaching is ingrained and we willingly continue to pass the agency over our sovereignty to others; parents, teachers, government, partners, friends, "professionals", to do what they do for our "own good". We conform. This is not a modern phenomenon for women, but extends back through time, certainly as far back as Roman occupied Britain, who brought with them the New Religion of Christianity. Young women passed from their father's house to their husband's house. The Norman Conquests in England brought the rule that women were the property of the male Head of House, unless she was a widow. She, without means of her own, without autonomy, property or wealth (for any money she had earned or inherited and brought to the union became her husband's upon marriage). She, who was unable to make her own choices and decisions, or voice her opinion, deferred always to her husband.

Until the 15th century, women generally had no surname and when they married they became known as "... the wife of ...". By the 16th century the family surname was a recognised unit in societal norms with the children taking their father's name as theirs. The surname usually referred to the place from where they lived or the Head of House's occupation or his father's ie Davidson from David's son or MacDonald meaning the son of Donald. The "wife" however, still possessed nothing of her own and women were now starting to express a desire to keep their own birth name. Such radical notions were not encouraged and were barely acknowledged as the patrilineal family surname continued through subsequent generations as a mark of status. A man's legacy was his family name.

In Scotland however, things were different. Dr Dauvit Horsbroch, of the *Scots Language Centre*, explains in *The Scotsman* newspaper how Scots women traditionally kept their own surname after marriage:

"It was always the custom in Scotland – and still so in legal terms today – that a woman does not lose her family name as in England, but continued to be known after marriage by her own name...
This custom reflects the strength of kith, kin and family... the concept that a man often joined his wife's kin group rather than simply the other way around."

Despite Scotland's patriarchal society, the women were considered a fiery, able and gutsy lot, particularly those of the 18th century. Post 1746 when the Jacobite rebellion failed to reinstate the Catholic House of Stuart to the throne, the Protestant Hanoverian rule was the order of the way and Highland life and culture was hence forth exterminated and brought under the British standard. You would think that the papal populous would be less liberal and more conservative in their expectations of how woman ought to behave, but no. It was Victoria's reign in the 19th century which stripped any lingering remnants of sovereignty and decreed what was lady-like and proper, leaving the women of the 19th century with less rights and sovereignty than their 18th century great-grandmothers. It was during this time that the accepted recognition of a woman was by her married name, her husband's name, north of the border. Whether Scots women relinquished their name and independence for societal expectation, proprietary or for romance is unclear. What is interesting however, is that when women die, married or not, it is their own name, their maiden name, that is engraved on their headstone. So they do reclaim their own name in their own right, just a shame it's after they have passed...

The tradition of a woman being given an engagement ring came to being as it showed that she belonged to her husband-to-be, (thanks for that tradition goes to the Romans) but handily it also meant she had something of worth that she could sell in a hurry for money if need be, or if her fiancé broke off the engagement, thus leaving her potentially undesirable for future wedded bliss and financial security. You'll notice that there is no such tradition for men's engagement rings. Wedding rings for men are a modern take, coming into fashion only during the Second World War, when the ring was a symbolic connection to their love back home.

Today's woman still are not viewed as sovereign when it comes to making decisions for our own bodies. See who is making decisions on our behalf, for women's healthcare and women's rights in government, it's the menfolk by a significant majority! At time of writing 220 MPs of the 650 elected MPs in Westminster are female (33%, meaning 67% are men; 45% are women in the Scottish Parliament, 48% in National Assembly for Wales and 30% in Northern Ireland Assembly).

The more we delegate our adult sovereignty the lesser the connection we have to ourselves, to our intuition, to belief in ourselves, and the easier we are to manipulate or influence. Obviously not all those who are in possession of our sovereignty are exercising it for malicious means, sometimes it is a friend or relative who doesn't know any better. Does it make it right? Of course not, it's a toxic situation and potentially tricky to navigate. Sovereignty that has been assumed by another and taken without your consent, perhaps an abusive partner or narcissistic parent is more difficult still and not a quick fix, this is something you may need professional guidance with. Recognising this is the first step in reclaiming your personal sovereignty. I don't for one second think it will be a easy process or without ugliness or messiness. It will absolutely be challenging and take every ounce of strength and determination, but it will be worth it, mess and all.

It may be a terrifying concept perhaps to consider yourself with so much power and self confidence. It may make you want to shrink back into yourself, but go gently, baby steps here. Alternatively you may feel angry, frustrated and energised to boldly step in your personal power NOW. Just sit with the feelings you have in this moment. Feel them and notice how your body is reacting. How does your heart feel? Is it racing? How does your stomach feel? Is it tight or got butterflies? What is your head and inner voice telling you? Look at why and be honest. If you can't be honest with yourself then when can you and with whom?

I am not suggesting that every woman needs to be Boudicca or Scáthach. My intention with encouraging you to re-establish yourself as a sovereign being in your own right, is to redress the inequality that still exists today, the double standards and expectations placed on women, and to remind you of the wonder of who you are, in all your glory. I want you to trust yourself, reconnect with your intuition and imagination, confidence and self belief, all unapologetically; why should you ever apologise to anyone for being yourself? Don't censor your personality, or quieten your voice to make someone else more comfortable. Keeping silent makes you compliant not sovereign. You have plenty of your own opinions and the flexibility to change these as you learn and grow and experience life. You have free will and both a right and a need to exercise it. Doing so in a way that aligns with your integrity and sense of self, your sacred sovereign self.

Sovereignty is dignity.

Whichever way this matter of sovereignty has caught you, it is worth remembering that knowledge is power and knowing the history of female sovereignty is important.

Pre Roman invasion and pre Christianisation of the British Isles, this was a land where the people honoured and revered local deities, most of whom were in the form of a goddess. The land was considered to be the feminine divine (Goddess). SHE was not an entity in the heavens, SHE was the land itself and because of this, the land was Sovereign, meaning that no-one owned it. The people lived on the land, worked it and took care of it; *they* belonged *to* the land. When a new King was crowned he had to marry the land in sacred ceremony. His right to rule was determined and granted by the Goddess via a sacred consummation with a priestess selected on the Goddess's behalf. His right to rule was at HER discretion and he agreed to ensure the continued protection of the land. Should he fail in his duty he was promptly replaced.

Women were held in equal regard to men; they were judged by skill and choices, could be and were fierce warriors, leaders of their tribe/clan, owned property, chose whom to marry and were able to divorce, were sexually liberal as they chose their partners, she named her children, not their father. Women were sovereign because they were in control of their own choices and were respected as such.

Sovereignty is sacred.

The stories and legends of the old ways were kept by oral tradition. When Christianity arrived to our shores it was, over the passing of time, pretty easy to reduce and diminish the Goddess and the role of women through the retelling of myths through their patriarchal eyes and written accounts. The Christian monks wrote of the truth, their truth, and to them the truth was God, only God, never tainting their vellum with such heresy as documenting a Goddess, heaven forbid! She became no more than a faery queen in tales for children. As the centuries rolled over, the skills and knowledge passed down through the generations, such as folk medicine and women's health (i.e. menstruation, childbirth, menopause), were to be feared, taken over, dominated and controlled by the more important men folk. Women were now in competition with one another. Jealousy over men was encouraged, distrust was rife and gossip was entertainment. Isn't it interesting how knowledge of plant medicine and remedies was the work of wicked wanton witches yet medicine, ill informed / ill judged practice of surgery and procedures was of course perfectly sensible because science and man? Valuable and necessary attributes usually associated with women such as nurturing, empathy and the ability to show emotion were hence viewed as weaknesses rather than strengths.

This is not an anti-man war cry. This is us acknowledging the past and reasserting ourselves as whole, autonomous beings as is our birth right. Sovereignty understands the balance of nature, equilibrium and knowing that in each of us resides both masculine and feminine energy, neither better or worse than the other. Our true selves are living, breathing creatures experiencing the world we live in, in which ever way we can, and maybe, we can do it differently from how we have been taught to. Can we look to our ancestors and learn from them? Can we look within to see what we know and want, and check where our balance is out of kilter?

Your inner Wild is your sovereignty. They are one and the same, you can't have or be one without the other. Understanding what wild means to you will go a long way in the awakening of your own inner Wild.

Wild, in my opinion, is simple, is essential, is paired back, raw and honest. To awaken our Wild, we need to reconnect with that simplicity, with our body and reconnect with the wisdom and knowings within; those memories, cellular memories and ancient wisdoms in your bones.

My interpretation of wild is:

something in its natural state – untamed, uncaged, uncontrolled, fiercely positive, primal and true.

Who is Wild?

Wild is the Maiden, the Mother & the Crone.

I hear wild and I feel excited and energised. Everyone is wild at their core but not everyone knows how to or wants to release and rewild it. I wonder, what emotions or reactions does the word **wild** evoke in you? Is it a state of being? Is it a personality trait? Is it a lifestyle? Is it to be feared or revered? Is it something you are (or are not)? Is it an *it* or maybe a *her/she*? In a world of love 'n' light and being good, how wild are you and how tame have you become?

I know I'm asking many questions, but how can we awaken something within if we don't know who or what it is, and understand what it means or how it feels?

Awakening and rewilding lies not with the external elements but inner values. Knowing and, more importantly, living and honouring these values on a daily basis is where true rewilding takes place. It is a journey establishing personal boundaries, taking a hard look in the mirror at your ~~flaws~~ imperfections, and accepting or rejecting what fits or doesn't, as well as confronting your past, your beliefs and your actions. The path is a never ending spiral; the journey, wild.

Your journey and path to this point and beyond has been and will be different from mine, because it's yours, and so too is your knowing of Wild.

2

Know Yourself

To know thyself is the beginning of wisdom.
*~ Aristotle or Socrates
(both credited with quote) ~*

Before we reawaken our inner Wild I need to ask, who are you? The real deep down you. Do you know or even remember? The you that you are in your mind, that is your authentic you. Who is the you without the roles you've been assigned or the titles you bear? Does your outward identity mirror your inner self? Is the you that is projected the one you've been told you should be or who you truly are? Maybe you know who you are and are completely comfortable in yourself. It may be you know who you are but keep certain bits hidden because of fear or shame or because that's not the you you're supposed to be. Perhaps you haven't lost who you are, but are taking the opportunity to (re)claim who you really are!

Who are you? Well, that very much depends upon who and when you ask, doesn't it? You will be labelled differently depending upon the the role you are playing at any given point. Daughter or mother or friend or student or employee or an inspiration or a lovely person or a pain in the arse or all of the above in one day. There will be whole list of different labels to identify you by, but that list is very one dimensional and changes constantly. It doesn't really mean anything. You are not your labels and you don't have to define yourself to anyone. What is important is remembering that you are more than the roles you play. Knowing who you are means you won't allow your identity to be defined by other people's opinions. Taking on the identity prescribed or expected by others means you are delegating your sovereignty and as such will act in accordance with and to the standard expected.

The more you learn, be it about life or yourself, the more you evolve and grow and I suppose, change. A good few years ago now, a then-friend said to me "You've changed." I disagreed with the "change" part as I didn't think I had actually changed as such, more remembered who I was and in honouring my true self, I sought out more to learn to expand my knowledge and understanding. I was pleased she had noticed. However, the comment was not meant as a compliment.

The only thing growing in stagnation is toxicity.

I find myself returning to this "you've changed" comment (complete with the visual in my head of her facial expression) time and time again. I am not the same person I was 5, 10, 15, 20 years ago, and I very much doubt that I will be the same person in 5 years time - and thank goodness for that. I don't want to stagnate.

Our blueprint of who we are, lies unchanged underneath all the layers of crap we have accumulated since childhood, through our teens, twenties, thirties and beyond. As we find out about and learn new things, have new experiences, try new ideas, discover what we like and dislike, our journey to who we are really, gets both closer and further away from that blueprint.

How do we rediscover this blueprint? By taking the necessary time and making space for ourselves, turning inwards to nurture ourselves and really get to know ourselves better. This is deep work, not naval gazing narcissism, but with purpose and deliberation. It is free from judgement and shame and it is not meant to be shared with anyone else; you don't need their input at this stage. It is about finding out for yourself who you are. You may reconnect with yourself in remembering your roots and ancestry or perhaps your wild sovereignty lies in your release from familial traditions, cycles and possibly trauma. We can reclaim who we truly are when we are honest and strip away all the "shoulds" and expectations, when we are no longer swayed or influenced by the opinions and judgements of others, well intentioned or otherwise.

Knowing who we are when we look at the surface or the bits we 'like' is easy. We can, I hope, all think of at least one thing we like about ourselves or think of something we are good at, but really tapping into the true self also requires knowing, embracing, releasing and accepting our shadow self. The bits we don't like, or cause us pain. It's all part of our make up. For instance, I know I am too much for some people; I verbally overcompensate when I'm nervous, I am incredibly judgemental and have obnoxious tendencies. I can be a bit of a show off after a glass of vino or two, yet confrontation averse and really hard on myself, to the point of hating myself through sheer frustration, when situations come up, comments are made and I don't say anything at the time. It is an absolute truth that just because I didn't react to a particular situation does not mean I didn't notice. I may forgive, but I certainly don't forget. I'm a fucking elephant! And an observant one at that.

It is an interesting journey, this thing we call life, unravelling who we are and who we have come to be. It can be difficult to look at why you are the way you are and identifying the roots of certain characteristics or traits. Cringing and feeling shame or embarrassment at previous actions or mistakes is part of this undertaking. You can't change the past, it helped shape who you are today, but it doesn't define you. In order to move on, you have to face the past, acknowledge it, feel the feels and let it go. Far easier said than done. I know! But it's a vital step if knowing yourself wholly is important to you.

The part I struggle with the most, is being my authentic self with others. Depending on whose company I am in, will depend on which part of me is out in the open. I guess part of it is trust. The people/parent pleaser in me worries about being honest and true in case of offending others or not being taken seriously or being misunderstood. I am really trying to take on the advice that other people's opinions of me are none of my business. That is a challenge. But I'm getting there.

It is easy in this period of temporary isolation that we are all living in, to lose ourselves, even a little bit. Our usual anchors that either ground us or remind us of who we are, as in the titles we hold or the roles we play, are no longer part of our everyday existence. Our rhythms and routines have shifted or disappeared altogether. Some of us embrace this period of quietude, some of us enjoyed the novelty of it initially but now the shine is beginning to tarnish and some us are all at sea. But remember in amongst all the chaos that is swirling around the globe currently, there is you, unwavering and standing strong, whether only in soul or in person too; testament to all that you have learned up until this very point, all that got you to here.

Be true to you, not anyone else.

So you know who you are, but what about where you come from? Does that matter? I think it does. We each have our own cultures where we live or grew up that are rich in their history, traditions, folklore and language. Your ancestral DNA is imprinted in your very fabric of existence. You create and tell your own stories, but what can you learn from the past for today and moving forward? How can you weave the stories of your ancestors into yours? Do you want to?

The blood of the ancestors flows through you veins.
Memories held deep in your soul.

Did you know that we are born with all our eggs already present in our ovaries; the egg that became me was already in my mother at the time of her birth which means that part of what was to become me was already within my own grandmother. Just like the Russian Matryoshka, meaning "little maiden", or Babushka, meaning "elderly woman or Grandmother", dolls which represent the matrilineal lineage. The baby doll inside the mother inside the grandmother and so on, mirroring our own grandmother line. I never got to know my maternal Gran but so love hearing about her and asking my mum questions about her mother and her life.

To accept what you cannot change or to change what you cannot accept?

Acceptance is the balance in this exercise of getting to know your inner self without experiencing an existential crisis. It comes in a variety of guises. Acceptance of self, of others, of situations and circumstance. I know who I am (or at least I do at this moment in time). This past year or two I have been swimming deep in the waters of my shadow, uncovering and exposing the bits I'd rather not face and would prefer to remain submerged. There are parts of my physical body I like and dislike, there are parts of my character I like and dislike, but I accept that these collectively, the good, the bad, the positive and the negative, are the parts that make me, *me*. Of course I am a work in progress, continually trying, failing, succeeding, learning, trying again, growing and evolving. It is a never ending process. And it starts with accepting who I am. This is the foundation upon which everything else is built; personality, values, opinions, boundaries and probably more. Accepting, liking and loving ourselves is not vanity, it's sanity. You, me, we, are unique, beautifully whole, imperfectly perfect and enough, right now as we live and breathe. So let us celebrate who are are rather than beat ourselves up about who we are not and stop comparing ourselves to others.

You are you and no-one else.

Regardless of "beliefs" I think the most important one we have is in ourselves. Be your own biggest supporter and let your light shine for all to see. I believe in me. How about you? Where does self acceptance sit in your process? Are you a work in progress too or yet to start or serenely accepting of your acceptance?

3

Values & Boundaries

Different doesn't mean wrong.
It means different.
~ Lissa Corra ~

How do you know what your values are? Actually, before you define what your personal values are, we should probably start with identifying what a value is in the first place. Essentially your values are a collection of rules that set your moral compass. They allow you to decide the difference between what you believe to be right or wrong, identify characteristics or behaviours you feel drawn to or repelled by. They allow you to make judgements and difficult decisions, helping you to know what it is that you deem important and acceptable to you. They provide a framework to guide you when setting your boundaries, basically aiding you as you chart your course through life.

There are different types of values that we hold; family values that we grew up with, societal values that are culturally indoctrinated, political values that we align with as we take to the ballot box, and spiritual values that we connect with in our chosen path. The most important values however are the collection of personal ones that we each hold dear to ourselves, which are as unique to us as our fingerprints. They belong to and are decided upon by each individual irrespective of family, peer or cultural opinion.

Deciding on what your personal or core values are is not just a case of sitting down and picking from a big list of approved values. They are instilled from childhood, where some values will stay with you for a life time and others will be tweaked and adjusted to better suit as you develop and grow inline with your experiences and some will be rejected completely and replaced with alternatives that reflect the person you are at that time. It is a constantly evolving process. Perhaps sitting down for an annual review of our values would be a better use of our time rather than creating fallible New Years Resolutions?

> *Your beliefs become your thoughts,*
> *your thoughts become your words,*
> *your words become your behaviour,*
> *your behaviour become your habits,*
> *your habits become your values*
> *and your values become your destiny.*
> ~ *Mahatma Gandhi* ~

Knowing what your values are and where they have come from is crucial when figuring out what is actually important to you, right here, right now. As does knowing which values are your non-negotiables. (There are two exercises at the end of this thread to help you discern your values and their priorities.) The reason for this ties in beautifully with your sovereignty; your choices made, which are founded in your beliefs and your actions taken, determine who you are, what you stand for and form your identity, at this time. Are you consciously creating your identity or conforming to the appropriate and acceptable notion of identity?

One of my core values centres on trust and truth. Is this one of yours? What is trust? Is *it* a feeling, an emotion? Is *it* an instinct? *It* is certainly built up over time and through experience. *It* can be a split second decision to throw caution to the wind and decide to trust or place blind faith in something greater e.g. religion. I believe trust is something we place in others, in ourselves and in situations. *It* is earned yet can be lost in a single moment. *It* can be taken for granted. Can *it* ever be regained once broken or will *it* always have fracture lines?

As we have established, we each have our core values and beliefs but did you realise that there are some we hold as truths? They are ours and ours alone. We cannot expect anyone else to adhere to these as they will have their own set of values. There may be a cross over and similarities, but just as each person is particular to themselves, so too are their truths, their perception of the truth and their trust in their own truth. When they don't align, we have to decide if relationships and friendships can work around the difference or whether they cannot, and instead come to an impasse and dissolve.

Trust and truth are words and instincts many say they value. We generally want people to be honest and truthful. Post after post can be read all across the inter webs on every platform (and in this very book) about living in our truth, standing in our truth, trusting our intuition, trusting ourselves, but the truth of the matter is that that is scary! It can be deeply unpleasant to the point of uncomfortably ugly - what if you don't like or agree with the truth? Can you trust it? Can you trust yourself to handle the truth? (I'm hearing Jack Nicholson's voice in my head right now). Do you trust yourself to honour your truth when all others around are in opposition or don't understand? Can you trust the person delivering the truth; yourself or another?

To take that leap of faith and be bold and trust, whatever it is you need to trust, is to be brave and vulnerable. The essence of trust is in the vulnerability. You allow yourself to be vulnerable with another and trust them with that. I'm now hearing Brené Brown's voice in my head as I type:

Without vulnerability there is no trust!

How can you have one without the other? Simple, you can't. It doesn't work? Who do you trust? Who can you be vulnerable with? Are they the same people? And I think, the reason why once trust has been damaged it is so hard to repair it, is because we allowed ourselves to be open and let our guard down therefore it hurts so much when we feel we have been disregarded or betrayed.

I think too, the biggest trust we have to have is in ourselves. I don't see that we can fully trust another without fully trusting and believing in ourselves - despite what we might think! Being honest and truthful with ourselves first; to know who we are and what our values are will hold us steady when we are challenged or our boundaries are crossed. A truth for me is the desire to shy away from [avoid] confrontation as I don't like to hurt other people and I used to fear rejection, but I have learned that not trusting myself to face situations from a point of honesty has not protected others or me from hurt but rather hurt all concerned.

As uncomfy as it is, I have resolved within myself to trust myself and speak my truth no matter what, because anything less is simply me not respecting myself, my boundaries or my health. I'm not going to violate the trust I've placed in myself to make others feel better about themselves. Other people's reactions are not my responsibility nor yours. Obviously there is a point of not being mean and unkind just to be "truthful", there is nothing to be gained for anyone in that situation. I have trust that each person I come across will be accountable and responsible for their own actions, thoughts and opinions. And that's a truth! Do you agree? Feel free not to.

Alongside reclaiming our sovereignty and knowing our core values, we need to establish our boundaries and then the test; upholding them. This is possibly the hardest thing you will be asked to do in this book.
What do I mean by boundaries? I mean a limit that you have decided upon and is the lowest standard of acceptable behaviour you will tolerate. It may be in regards to your physical person, your mental and emotional energy, material possessions, your time and energy, personal space, your beliefs and values. For instance, you are a punctual person but have one friend who is always an hour late. Do you accept that that is just the way they are or is it disrespectful to you who shows up at the agreed time? You are organised and helpful, generally good at giving advice, a contrast to your sister who lives from one catastrophe to the next but knows it's fine because you've always got her back even though she never listens to your advice. Do you drop what you are doing to help solve her latest crisis when you are in the middle of one at home, therefore causing an argument with your partner? Your brother has lost his job and needs to borrow some money to help him out until he gets another job, but he hasn't paid back the last handout. Do you give him what he wants or remind him that he is still in debt to you from previous help but work out an alternative plan to solve the cash shortfall? Perhaps your boss is always giving you the more challenging tasks to do because they know that you will get the job done, while your colleague, who is paid the same, has a much smaller, less

burdensome, pretty easy workload. Is it worth upsetting the apple cart or do you just get on with it?

Only you can decided what you are willing to accept from others, and how many times. When you assert your boundaries it is absolutely paramount that you 1. communicate them and 2. maintain consistency.

How do you feel about being nice or being thought of a nice person? I'm not nice. It's not my goal to be nice. This is not how other people view me, I know plenty people who think I'm nice, but they only see one side of me. I have boundaries and a face for everyone. Being nice is exhausting and serves no-one. I'm not interested in nice. I want truth, honesty and authenticity. And integrity too. I've been a people pleaser for too long, and while I'm nowhere near as concerned with pleasing others as I used to be, I'm still a work in progress, unravelling the need to please and put others' comfort before mine to avoid awkwardness. Pleasing folk at the expense of personal boundaries or values is a recipe for bitterness and exhaustion, and, to be blunt, it's neither my job nor responsibility. If focusing on no longer trying to please, but rather on taking care of myself, on respecting my boundaries and on what's important to me instead means I'm not nice, well that's just fine by me. I'm not nice. I don't mean that I am horror, I'm generally peace and love but mostly boundaries. And they are becoming more defined and stronger all the time! I'm done with drama and other people's shitty behaviour. Not taking it, not making it better, living and let live on my own terms!

Boundaries are Respect.

That sounds sensible and straight forward but why then are boundaries so difficult to implement and maintain? What are the barriers to healthy boundaries? Elton John may very well sing about "Sorry" being the hardest word but I see his "Sorry" and raise him a "No". The number of people I have spoken to over the years, whether in work or to friends, who have real issues with saying the teeny tiny word "No" (myself included) is rather staggering. It seems to me to be an issue particularly prevalent with women. Why? Societal conditioning. That's why, in my humble opinion. We are guilted into saying YES when we really want to say NO and it is not restricted to one area of life either. The guilt is powerful and can be utilised, although not always intentionally, by our employers, our colleagues, our children, our partners, our parents, our extended families, our friends. The list goes on. Anyone with whom you have contact with can express a need and if you don't agree to meet that need, more often than not, guilt sets in. So what do we do? We say "Yes" and instead of feeling guilt, the emotions that may follow are resentment or begrudgement. Wonderful isn't it? To complete this vicious little cycle of not implementing healthy boundaries is that when we confess later on that really, we wanted to say "No", the other person asks why we didn't just say "No" at the time. Argh! And so it goes. I know this is not just me either. People pleasing is a thing, it's insidious and steals our sovereignty.

Being unable to say "No" or feeling really uncomfortable saying "No" is a classic example of an unhealthy boundary. Other unhealthy boundaries include:

- not communicating in the first instance what your expectations are,
- allowing others to continually abuse your boundaries, ignoring them altogether,
- constantly putting other people's needs before your own, even if it's making you unwell,
- trying to please too many people and pleasing none,
- not protecting your privacy and personal space,

including both online and in person, oversharing, especially with a stranger or with a new acquaintance,
- not respecting another person's boundary, physically or emotionally,
- carrying the weight of responsibility for others that is not actually yours to carry,
- not wanting to cause problems for others at the detriment to your personal sovereignty,
- acceptance of other's poor behaviour rather than holding them accountable,
- freely and willingly giving away your sovereignty to another for them to control, effectively shirking your own responsibilities.

So, what do healthy boundaries look like then? Well, they start with you knowing your rights: your right to be treated respectfully, the right to say no (and not feeling guilty about it), the right to value yourself as a priority, the right to make mistakes and learn from them (what are mistakes if not lessons?), as well as your right not to have to live up to someone else's expectation or standard.

Healthy boundaries to consider implementing if you haven't already, include :

- knowing what your own needs are; taking responsibility for yourself, your actions and having the self confidence to stand by your choice of action,
- saying "No" when you mean "No" and "Yes" when you mean "Yes",
- accepting that not every person who asks of you will want to hear "No" and may therefore feel rejected or go off in a huff. Remembering that they are responsible for their own reactions, regardless of what comes back. This is where your inner Wild

reigns supreme as the sovereign being you are. And it takes practice,
- consistency is your friend. Just like when teaching small children or puppies their boundaries, pushing or breaking the boundaries has consequences and then following though on the consequences. They do learn. Communicating your boundary and enforcing it, rinse and repeat as many times as necessary will get the message across. Someone honouring your set boundary is being respectful to you, crossing your set boundary (worse if repeat offender) has no respect. Harsh but true,
- respecting and protecting your privacy, your values, and your opinions,
- acknowledging and respecting other people's boundaries, including their "No",
- holding yourself and others accountable for actions rather than accepting poor behaviour,
- walking away from relationships or friendships than are toxic, disrespectful or harmful in any way. Knowing too that you do not require their permission to leave.

The positive benefits of having firm boundaries that are aligned with your values and your sovereignty affect not only your mental health but also your physical health and personal safety, your confidence, your ability to make important decisions and the enjoyment of your life.

4

Remember Reconnect Reclaim

Meditation

Inner Wild Reveal

Before we go into our meditation, I'd like you to pause for a moment and just breath normally, and ask yourself how do you feel in your body? How do you feel about your body, the bits you like and those you don't and why that is so. How do you feel about being a woman at this time? In order to know any of that we need to move our body and feel into it. Where does your breath go when you inhale? How does it travel, how does it feel? Where does it come from when you exhale, how does it sound? How does your body want to move? (pause for a couple of breaths and just observe them)

We are going to awaken your inner Wild Woman. Maybe you know her as Shakti or Kundalini but I call her Wild.

We start this meditation standing, feet hip width apart, or wider if comfortable and close your eyes. Keeping your knees soft and slightly bent, gently begin to move your hips, sway side to side or in a circle, it makes no difference, just feel into it. Allow your arms to move, maybe sink down into your knees or stretch out tall and long. We are moving out of your head space and into your body and energetic space. How does your body feel now? Don't force the movement, just relax and let it happen, be guided by your body's want and need to move, in time with the natural rhythm of your breath. Allow your body to freely move. No thinking just moving.

When you are ready, place your hands over your heart. On next inhale, breathe deeply and directly into your heart space and feel it expand. As you exhale throw your arms wide and exhale right through to and out of the tips of your fingers. We will do that again on the next breath. Feel the breath, the expansion and the release.

If comfortable, take a deeper, wider stance in your knees. Place your hands over your pelvic bowl. On your next inhale breathe deeply down into your womb space. Feel it expand and energise. As you exhale throw your arms wide and sink lower into your knees and release that breath out through your mouth, ahhhhhhhhhhhhh!!!! Notice the sound of its release. We will do that again – breath into your inner cauldron, feel the power, exhale that breath and keep it going for as long as you can.

And now just breathe. You can stay standing or may wish to sit down. Keep your eyes closed.

Imagine you are standing in front of a full length mirror. Take in the vision you see. Who is looking back at you? Do you recognise her? How does she look? What expression is on her face? Look into her eyes – what are they saying to you? Focus on and connect with those eyes, they are your portal into her soul. (pause for a couple of breaths)

Shift your gaze now down to her heart. Can you sense its beat or any emotion held there? Does it glow with any particular colour? Breathe into that heart space, connect with the reflection. (pause for a breath). What is her heart telling you? What is her soul's truth? What does she care about most? Who or what does she love? Is there any pain needing to be acknowledged, released and let go? Is her heart free or caged? (pause for as long as you need). Do you notice any changes in the heart area since you first gazed upon her reflection? (pause for a breath)

Move your gaze further still, now down to her pelvis, holding her womb space within. Can you feel or read the energy there? Does it glow with any particular colour? This is the centre of creation, of her creativity, the seat of her soul. (pause for a breath) What messages are you receiving from the depths of her womb – is this the home and birth place of her Wild? What lights her up? What gets her juices flowing? Is there any stagnation needing released or any blockages needing recognised or removed? How is her energy flowing? Stay here and breathe into the space. Feel it (pause for as long as you need). Do you notice any changes at all? (pause for a further breath)

Bring your focus back out and take in the vision of the woman standing before you. Does she look any different to when you first gazed upon her? How do you feel looking at her now? Do you know her? Do you know her better? Have you awoken your inner Wild? Have you seen your true inner Wild?

Look into her eyes. Place your right hand over your heart and your left over your womb and breathe here, fully and deeply for 3 breaths as the mirror slowly fades away.

For the next few minutes feel free to move your body to ground yourself back into the present moment. You may also wish to journal anything that came up for you or just relax and focus on your breath.

Welcome back.

Journal Prompts

Ask yourself the following questions. See how they make you feel and answer them honestly. Take your time and see what comes up. These are not one-time asks either; ask them again after a period of time once you've completed the book, or after 6 months, a year, etc and see how/if your answers have evolved.

- **Awaken Your Wild You**. How does that sentence make me feel? Excited? Scared? Meh? And why is that?
- What does Wild mean or look like to me? Was my answer what I thought it would be?
- Do I have an inner Wild lying in wait for her time?
- What does Sovereign mean to me?
- What does my inner Wild want and need? How does she feel currently? Why?
- Is my inner Wild ready to awaken and rise?
- Is my Wild already awake?
- Being a sovereign woman, how does that feel in my physical body?

- How am I breaking free and rewilding myself?
- Do I feel tamed or hemmed in by modern life and societal obligations and standards?
- If I've never been tamed, how do I stay wild and sovereign?
- What is the energy of wild, is it masculine or feminine? How does it feel?
- Is Wild my vocal NO or is it my YES?
- Where in my life can I become more sovereign?
- Where in my life have I delegated my sovereignty? Why?
- Where am I standing in my own way to my sovereignty? Why?
- What and who runs through the blood in my veins?
- What ancient memories am I holding at a cellular level?
- Who are my ancestors, where were they from?
- Who am I and where am I from?
- What do I love about myself? How would a friend describe me?
- What makes me awesomely ME?
- How do I stay true to me?
- Why do I believe what I do, where does that belief come from?
- What are my true values? How did I decided that they are my values?
- How am I recognising and therefore honouring my values, or not, as the case may be?
- What does trust mean to me? How important is it to me?
- How do I feel when there is no trust or when a previous bond of trust has been broken?
- What are my personal boundaries? How do I feel when they are crossed? What do I do, or not do,

when they are crossed? How can I reinforce them if required?
- What are my barriers to implementing and maintaining my boundaries?
- What message am I sending out to the universe? What life am I manifesting? What reality am I creating for me? What version of me am I telling myself of?
- What am I creating, claiming, owning and transforming?
- What story am I writing about myself?

Action

- Write a letter to your younger self at the threshold of adult life. Share insights, advice, stories, memories and anything else you need to get off your chest.
- Write a letter to yourself in the present. Write down all the things, situations, conversations that you have experienced that have left their mark on you whether it be residual shame, guilt, remorse, regret, longing, disappointment (insert any other negative emotion) and ask yourself for forgiveness. You can't move on when your past still has a hold of you. Face it and release it. This is not who you are now. Everybody makes mistakes but they don't define you if you don't let them.
- Write a letter to yourself in the present. Write down all the things, situations, conversations that you have experienced that have left their mark on you with love, joy, accomplishment, success, passion, pride, empowerment, inspiration, surprise (and any other positive emotion) and allow yourself to bask in the abundance of such beauty of all you have witnessed,

created, celebrated, appreciated and been a part of.
- Make a list without thinking about it too much, what are the attributes, characteristics, beliefs and behaviours that you value, then do the same for those that are the opposite. Now look at those 2 lists and see which is a true reflection of how you are living your life currently. Where could you make changes? Do certain values remain true values for you, or have they been hanging around just because?
- From the list of values you hold, break it down further – where did they come from: family, school, media, church, peers, politicians, personal experience. Now rank your values in priority of importance to you and what you stand for. Use this list for setting your goals in life, making hard decisions, confronting uncomfortable situations and living your best life.
- Ask a good friend who they think you are and see if the answers are the same as yours. **Only do this exercise once you have completed you own questions and inner work and are fully comfortable and sure in knowing who you are** – you don't want to be influenced and undo all your hard work.
- Research your family tree to see where you come from. This is particularly useful if older members of your family are no longer alive, alternatively ask the elder members of your family about their own memories and recollections of family stories, traditions, myths and legends.

THREAD TWO

CYCLES

***We are cycles within cycles.
Spiralling in perpetuity.
Never linear.***

~ Lissa Corra ~

5

Calendars ~ Seasons ~ Wheel of the Year

Live in each season as it passes; breathe the air, drink the drink, taste the fruit, and resign yourself to the influence of the earth.
~ Henry David Thoreau ~

Time, it's a funny old thing isn't it? It seems to never stand still, passes quickly or unbearably slowly. It can be measured in a number ways; by the passing of night into day into night, from month to month or season to season, counting seconds, minutes, centuries, millennia. We celebrate the passing of our own time by honouring our birthdays (a modern occurrence, in ancient times people knew how old they were by how many summers they had been alive, rather then an exact date of birth) and anniversaries. We are told that that time waits for no man and that it marches on, always moving forward. But is that true? Does time move in a linear fashion or is it a perpetual cycle; spring to summer, to autumn, to winter, to spring? Or can it do both, continually cycling within the continuum?

You may wonder why I'm questioning the concept of time in relation to your wilding, so allow me to explain. We are a part of the whole shebang, the universe, the cosmos, the earth, we are all connected to each other and to nature, we are impacted by and have an impact upon everything that happens in this spark of life, consciously or not. As a result, what we experience affects how we view events. Our remembering of the past, assimilating into the present and our choice of action is a direct result of something that happened at a specific moment in time. We learn time and time again as we cycle through different phases of life, the lessons that need learning. We have experiences that allow us to let go and release old patterns and habits. We relive the same moments repeatedly but always from a slightly different perspective due to the experiences lived and gained in the previous cycle(s).

Let us look at how time is measured, as I am curious to see how it fits, or doesn't fit with how you live your life or how you find your own personal rhythm in these cyclic spirals.

The first calendar that was the "official" way to date time by individual days and months was the Julian calendar, so named for Julius Caesar and came into use in 46BC. There were previous incarnations of annual calendars and keeping time which we will explore, but Caesar formalised the one we know and refer to as the Julian calendar. In that version February marked the end of the year and March 25th began the New Year. The Julian calendar was in use until the present day Gregorian calendar (named for Pope Gregory XIII), gradually came into use, replacing the Julian version, from 1582. Great Britain formally adopted the new calendar 1752. The last day of the old calendar was Wednesday 2nd September, and the following day was Thursday 14th September. The difference was a loss of 11 days and the New Year would then follow in January instead of March – hence why *Septem*, meaning 7, is now our 9th month, and *Octo*, meaning 8, is our 10th etc. The new Gregorian calendar adjusted the measure of time to move with the solar year and planetary alignment.

Then there is the other calendar, the much debated Celtic Ogham (pronounced Oh-am) calendar. Did the ancient Druids recognise the passing of each annual cycle by a cleverly organised calendar of 13 months, each 28 days long, named after the native trees and shrubs of this island? Or did Robert Graves, the English Poet, create this calendar in the 20th century from an old poem where he made a contrived, tenuous link between the Irish Celtic Ogham alphabet and the lunar months to quench the thirst of neo pagans in need of a nature based calendar? Does it matter? Personally, I like the Ogham calendar with its meaning behind the name of each month, however, it doesn't fit neatly into the annual shaped box with its 13 moons and very quickly falls out of alignment of moons within the prescribed months, and within a single year, which is frustrating.

In time before the Gregorian or Julian calendars with set dates and days, the passage of time was measured by the solar and lunar cycles, and acknowledged with the passing seasons. Much simpler, much more in tune with what was happening in the natural world.

When it comes to working with calendars for 21st century living, I use a combination of standardised Gregorian, especially when making plans or appointments and such with other people, but my diary/planner follows the lunar cycle, each new month begins on the New Moon, and finishes on the Dark Moon. These Moon months are numbered through the course of the year, beginning with the first New Moon in January. Some people prefer to use the New Moon around Samhain, and we will look at why further on in the chapter.

Monthly Calendar

Julian	Gregorian	Ogham
(1) Martius (New Year begins on 25th)	(1) January	(1) Birch 24th Dec - 20th Jan
(2) Aprilis	(2) February	(2) Rowan 21st Jan - 17th Feb
(3) Maius	(3) March	(3) Ash 18th Feb - 17th Mar
(4) Lunius	(4) April	(4) Alder 18th Mar - 14th Apr
(5) Quintilis	(5) May	(5) Willow* 15th Apr - 12th May
(6) Sextilis	(6) June	(6) Hawthorn 13th May - 9th Jun
(7) September	(7) July	(7) Oak 10th Jun - 7th Jul
(8) October	(8) August	(8) Holly 8th Jul - 5th Aug
(9) November	(9) September	(9) Hazel 5th Aug - 1st Sept
(10) December	(10) October	(10) Vine/Bramble 2nd Sep - 29th Sep
(11) Ianuarius	(11) November	(11) Ivy 30th Sep - 27th Oct
(12) Februarius	(12) December	(12) Reed 28th Oct - 23rd Nov
		(13) Elder 24th Nov - 23rd Dec

*This month is also known as the time of Women's Mysteries.

If we to go back to ancient, pre Roman, Britain, our calendar was in alignment with two seasons; summer and winter. Summer began when the hawthorn blossomed. Summer ended with the fall in temperatures and the first frosts. And so the cycle continued. The seasons were not determined by a set date, but by the weather and a close connection to the land.

At some point, the year was further split into the four distinct seasons we know today, spring, summer, autumn and winter. With the seasons come their festivals and celebrations. Differing opinions for when the seasons shift and the confusion between the myths and legends of how the ancients acknowledged the turning of the cyclic year are plentiful. There is of course no proof of what is right and correct, we can only surmise based upon archaeological remains, folkloric tales and trying to piece it together.

At different points in time, different celebrations were honoured to recognise the seasonal changes. Summer and summer's end (winter), as already mentioned, was one way, as was the acknowledgement of the dark half of the year and light half, the defining points being the equinoxes of spring and autumn. The Neolithic (latter end of stone age) people from around 4500BC used the sun as their guide, as evidenced by henges and stone circles. The most well known henge being Stonehenge in England, dating from around 2500BC where archaeological finds and carbon dating provide us with evidence of feasting and celebration at the Winter Solstice (not the Summer Solstice as is customary today) mostly likely in prayer and relief for the return of the life force; the sun. Over the course of the Bronze Age, the solar observations fell out of fashion and, by 1200 BC Iron Age Celts had arrived in Britain. They were guided not by the skies but by the land. They were warriors and farmers whose agricultural lifestyle gave forth to the four Quarter Days; Imbolc, Beltane, Lughnasadh and Samhain. The legends of Druids (who were allegedly Celtic) holding great ceremony at Stonehenge at Summer Solstice don't hold any water. There are some people who believe that the Druids were pre-Celtic natives of this island and therefore did indeed use the standing stones across the British Isles for rituals. Without any written documentation and the only witness accounts coming from the Romans via their own interpretation and propaganda towards the 'uncivilised natives', there are no 100% facts or anything close to, so we have to go on our own interpretations and understandings. (Remember my recommendation in the introduction, question everything and every source – I cannot impress enough how researching and finding out for yourself is necessary to know what is true for you.)

The 18th century saw a revival in Celtic heritage and history. Reconstruction groups were becoming popular in the 19th century, which is where we first see the combination of the four solar festivals and the four agricultural festivals. The eight festivals, renamed Sabbats, became cemented in neo-pagan spirituality by Gerald Gardener when he created Wicca in 20th Century and named The Wheel of the Year, which is followed by many Pagans the world over, Wiccan or not.

Seasonal Calendar
(Northern Hemisphere)

	Meteorological	Astronomical	Folk	Celtic
SPRING	1st March	Spring Equinox (21st March)	Imbolc (1st February)	n/a
SUMMER	1st June	Summer Solstice (21st June)	Beltane (1st May)	Beltane
AUTUMN	1st September	Autumn Equinox (21st September)	Lughnasadh (1st August)	n/a
WINTER	1st December	Winter Solstice (21st December)	Samhain (31st October)	Samhain

For me the true months of the seasons are January (winter), April (spring), July (summer), and October (autumn).

The Wheel of the Year recognises the eight seasonal festivals of both the sun and the earth that keep us connected to the changing season with each revolution. They are now referred to as the Quarter Days (Solar, considered to be of masculine energy); the two Equinoxes and two Solstices, interspersed by the Cross Quarter Days, formerly the Quarter Days, (earth based fire festivals, also called lunar festivals as may be celebrated at the nearest appropriate lunation, considered to be of feminine energy); Imbolc, Beltane, Lughnasadh and Samhain. Depending upon which calendar you follow, or where you live in the world, will depend where your seasons begin and end. The Wheel diagram overleaf shows the cycle for the northern hemisphere. The southern hemisphere has Lughnasadh in February, Autumn Equinox in March, Samhain in May, Winter Solstice in June, Imbolc in August, Spring Equinox in September, Beltane in October and Summer Solstice in December.

In the modern Wheel, the dates for each of these festivals are equally spaced out, roughly six weeks apart as we roll from one festival to the next. However, in ye olde days, the Cross Quarter days were acknowledged and celebrated by not only the weather but also by the nearest either Full Moon or Dark Moon (again, there is no written evidence to 'prove' this, but it makes sense due to lack of formal calendar).

Each festival, known as a Sabbat in Wicca, is celebrated over a 3 day period, commencing at sunset on the first day until sunset on the third day, i.e. Imbolc is celebrated 1st February, so it begins sunset 31st January until sunset 2nd February. While the actual celebration spans 3 days, the energy and connection to the season lasts the duration until the next festival.

Where the year starts and finishes in this perpetually cycling spiral of seasons is another point of debate. There is one school of thinking that appears to be the most mainstream in the spiritual world, whereby the Celtic New Year begins with Samhain. The logic behind this is due to the new day beginning at bed time; the evening is the start, therefore, Samhain is the twilight festival before the darkness of Solstice. Again, this is merely speculation. Winter Solstice has also been touted as New Year as has Spring Equinox (remember that the new year in the Julian calendar was March 25th) and Beltane. There is no right or wrong answer as to when it "officially" is, so it makes no difference when you choose to begin your cycle, if you follow the Wheel.

My own take on setting the calendar has been trial and error over the years, figuring out what makes sense and feels right with where I live. In my practice, my new year begins at the end of the Yuletide celebrations, in accordance with 31st December, Hogmanay. January is a period of rest and hibernation with the first festival being Imbolg. Imbolg is still winter time here in Central Scotland, but there are signs of stirrings under foot with the flowering of the snowdrops and crocuses. Springtime and the 3 other seasons fall in line with the astronomical calendar. Although, in 2020 I did feel the change in the seasons. Autumn arrived well before the Equinox, in fact it was blowing in at the start of August, which in more in time with the old Folk calendar. I will be paying close attention to the seasons this year to see if the threshold from one to the next remains astronomically on time or if it has shifted back to the old ways. See, there is no right or wrong, just trusting yourself to connect to the land around you and feel what's happening, to know where you are.

Wheel of the Year

- Winter Solstice
- Imbolc
- Spring Equinox
- Beltane
- Summer Solstice
- Lughnasadh
- Autumn Equinox
- Samhain

Looking at the Wheel of the Year and the seasons a bit closer now, we will journey through a full cycle and as you go along, I recommend that you cultivate your own rituals, practices and observances that you can revisit each year and reflect on the previous one. And perhaps create new traditions.

Imbolc

Pronounced "*Im*-olk" Imbolc (Irish Gaelic), Imbolg (Scots Gaelic) meaning "in the belly" and Oimelc, meaning "ewe's milk".

31st January - 2nd February

As the light lengthens, so the cold strengthens.

February; the month that welcomes in Imbolg and the first stirrings and whisperings of Spring, yet here in this part of the Northern Hemisphere, winter still holds us close. The days remain cold and there is still the possibility for snow, but the light is lengthening and the snowdrops and crocuses are in flower.

Imbolg is one of the least celebrated of the eight seasonal markers to be honoured in the natural year. This is possibly due to people not understanding its significance or unsure of the associations with milk. So what on earth is Imbolc? Depending upon your point of view, Imbolg represents the start of spring, the inbetweeny time between winter and spring, or it is considered be to very much a winter festival with spring still a while off yet. At this time the ewes are lactating, the ancients had milk once more and deep in the belly of mother nature, life is stirring and awakening. This is a festival of renewal and purification and as such, a far more appropriate time for making and sticking to new resolutions and goals. January is still very much a time of hibernation, darkness and heavy soul nourishing food not about diets and lack, but February with its slightly longer days and lightening evenings has a more sprightly feel, reflected both in the sky and in mood.

Imbolg is a fire festival which is very much feminine in its energy. All that is happening on and around Imbolg is happening here on and in the earth, Mother Nature, Gaia, The Great Mother. It is also the first festival in the cycle where the Maiden aspect of the Goddess is honoured. She is also known as Brigid, Bride, Brig and is associated with poetry, healing, fertility, fire energy (and skills relating to fire, home, hearth or forge), inspiration and muse. Imbolc is a beautiful time for women; mothers & daughters, friends, and female family members spending time together, perhaps learning a new skill or just enjoying being in one another's company, outwith the daily chores of home. There are many ways to honour this sacred time, whether you celebrate it from sunset on the Gregorian calendar date or around Lunar Imbolc (when the moon is a mere sliver of the new crescent, the witches new moon), or just when you *feel* the season start to shift; the actual calendar date is not important, there is no dogma dictating set times for the cross quarters, just do what feels right for you. Alternatively you may not consider Imbolc at all, and look upon Candlemas as a marker in your year, or you may not consider any marker as relevant and the start of February is the start of a new month as per any other.

This is the perfect time to start to move, to stretch, to wash the winter sleep from your eyes and begin your own stirring. What hopes, dreams, intentions and plans have you been tending and incubating through the winter's darkness that are now quickening and awakening? What is needing its final clean up before the spring? Are you looking to literally or metaphorically detox part of your life? What or who are you washing away and releasing? What skins are you shedding in these final weeks of winter? What truth or value are you remembering and reclaiming from underneath the tainted dirt and debris of patriarchy and society? This is the time to cleanse the outdated and the tarnished and make clean, clear space to welcome what's coming, to reclaim what you are bringing forth.

Spring Equinox

Vernal Equinox (meaning Spring time), also known as
Ostara (Germanic Goddess of Spring)
20th March - 22nd March

So many mists in March you see, so many frosts in May will be.

March; the month of rebirth, rejuvenation and re-emergence. Nature is reawakening all around; refreshed and revitalised. We leave behind the safety of winter's womb ready to re-emerge with fertile shoots of promise for abundance and prosperity. The dawn of a new future. The spring's sunbeams embrace us, our dreams and new beginnings. The sun is gaining in strength and length; joy and excitement ignite the air around us. This is the time to allow the buds of possibility to unfurl to bloom. The earth is fertile and the energy is rising, are you ready to step out into your own spring and reclaim who you are, what's yours, and see what flourishes?

The equinox is a time of balance. We have 12 hours of day light and 12 hours of darkness as the sun rises due east and sets due west; equal amounts of light and dark before we head on towards the solstice, with the increasing light.

This is the period of fertility; animals, nature, ideas and projects. Imagery of rabbits, hares, chickens and eggs symbolise the season's fertility. The rabbits and hares reputed for breeding, and the eggs, and chicks who lay eggs, represent the hatching of new life, birth (ever wondered what bunnies and chicks had to do with Christ's resurrection at Easter?). The equinox celebrates the Maiden aspect of the Goddess, of youth, enthusiasm, optimism and adventure. The legend of Ostara, or Eostre in particular, is where she carried a basket of brightly coloured eggs and was accompanied by her pet hare. As they travelled they brought forth new life and regeneration to the land scattering her coloured eggs amongst the flowers in the meadows.

The previous festival of Imbolg was embracing the last of

winter, and planning what was to come in the year ahead. This festival now calls upon us to put these plans into action. We got rid of the old and expired habits, practices and burdens in the previous cycle and are now ready to give new life to who and what we are to be, to what we have created, to what we are to birth. The energy is one of excitement, optimism and anticipation. As the year waxes, so too does our enthusiasm. The spring equinox mirrors a women's inner world in its Inner Spring season, where everything is new and fresh, preparing the fertile landscape, the pre-ovulation. It is also the waxing crescent moon phase. See how we are all connected ~ woman, nature, seasons, moon, our own inner cycles. All one.

How have you grown and evolved in the past revolution of the Sun? What loss have you grieved in preparation to be reborn or to re-emerge as your best and truest self? What are you birthing into the world this spring?

Beltane
Beltane meaning summer begins, Là Bealltainn (Scots Gaelic), Lá Bealtaine (Irish Gaelic)
30th April - 2nd May

Mists in May, heat in June, make the harvest come right soon.

May; the month of the May Queen, the start of country fetes and fairs with a maypole, and superstitious bad luck to couples who marry this month.

Traditionally, as the weather warmed, livestock was put out to the summer pastures. The masculine maypole was erected and inserted into the feminine earth and danced around in gaiety to raise the fertile energy of the land and loins. In my modern Scotland, May is usually when we have our summer; there are always two weeks in May that are gorgeous and hot, despite the auld wives warning:

Ne'er cast your clout til May be oot.

meaning don't put your winter jackets and jumpers away just yet, the weather could still surprise you with a cold snap.

The evening of 30th April (or at the point when the hawthorn bushes come into flower, or the nearest full moon) bonfires are built on the hilltops and these belfires are lit. The significance of the fire is that of purification where both beast and person walked between two fires to be sained (a specific, sacred, cleansing ritual for protection) in the smoke; cleansed and blessed through the smouldering juniper boughs. The transition through the gateway of winter into summer; for hope of a bountiful harvest, prosperity, good health and good luck for the people, for reproduction as well as fertility of the mind and soul. While the agricultural theme is not as important to the everyday person living in urban areas today, the celebration of summer and the fertility rites remain strong. Every year on 30th April, up on Calton Hill in Edinburgh the Belfire is lit and the celebration commences with a torchlit parade telling the story of the May Queen and the Green Man. It is truly spectacular with hundreds of participants in full costume and painted body art. (The last time I went it was freezing and poured with rain. I very much needed my jacket).

When the May Queen and the Green Man (Goddess and God/Consort) marry at the height of spring, their union brings forth new life. Là Bealltainn is an important celebration in the Pagan Calendar (Wheel of the Year); a time out of time, a magical time full of passion and promise with the warm, light nights guiding us into Summer.

Energy all around is rising. There is a sense of fun and joy in the air. In the autumn and winter we release, and allow the old habits and ideas and parts of us no longer in service to die off, but now in the late spring and awakening to summer we allow the new to flourish and grow, tending to the vulnerable shoots. We thrive in the light of the life force energy of the sun, which continues to wax and gain strength. This is the third festival of the Maiden archetype.

Beltane has equal importance in the calendar to Samhain, each forming a hinge into the next half of the cycle. At this hinge, the veil between this world and the other is gossamer fine, making it an excellent time to connect with our ancestors. It is also an important moment to connect to your inner feminine and masculine energies to unite them, not just from the point of fertility but also in love, especially for the love we have for ourselves. This is a very sensual time, express yourself, have fun.

Will you light the fire this evening and keep it burning until sunrise? Or perhaps rise with the sun and cleanse your face in the morning dew? What's firing your passion this Beltane? What do you want to achieve and grow and call into your life? What hopes and dreams will be conceived tonight in the sacred union of earth and sky?

As the sun sets,
the flames of the Belfires rise.
It's play time.
Farewell winter.
Welcome summer.
Abundant light,
joy and fertility most potent.
~ *Lissa Corra* ~

Summer Solstice
Litha, Midsummer
20th June - 22nd June

A wet June brings a dry September.

June; the start of summer, when all in the natural world is in full bloom and blossom. The air is charged with a sense of completion, success and fulfilment. In Scotland the school year is coming to a close for the summer holidays and for me personally, this June-born wummin completes her annual cycle around the sun and begins her next.

The solstice is the sun's climax, reaching its zenith, its maximum elevation in the sky. It has peaked in its journey. It is a pivotal moment when the the sun pauses in position before beginning its descent towards the lowest point at winter solstice. The pause provides us with the longest day and shortest night of the year. The culmination of the solar strength and consolidation of earthly gains. Bonfires are lit to add to the sun's strength (a form of sympathetic magic), despite there being no evidence of the ancients honouring the sun in this manner; it appears to be a 19th century creation. The purpose of the bonfires lit in ancient times were as a tool for protection rather than honour; the smoke cleansed and protected, and the cold ash fertilised the soil.

This is peak time of growth before the harvest. A bountiful harvest is required for survival through the winter. All customs and rituals are steeped in the land, protection and pleasing of the deity. This was less a celebration of the heavens and more a celebration of the people as this was also the time to get married. The full moon in June is referred to in these parts as the Honey Moon possibly due to the merriment of the occasion and drinking of the honey mead in celebration. The abundance of flowers in bloom made for the traditional bridal bouquet as the floral scent hid the tang of human odour as was due to the lack of regular soapy bathing. The Goddess is in her Mother phase now.

Enjoy the increasing warmth of the season, rejoice in the light, allow your self confidence to soar and appreciate the gifts of the present. This is the time to maximise your opportunities. That which is going on outside is a reflection of what is happening within, so celebrate your inner light and that of those around you. What alights your inner fire and burning passions? Which are the seeds you sowed in the spring that are now flourishing? What are you appreciating?

Lughnasadh
Pronounced *"Loo*-na-sahh", Lammas (meaning loaf mass)
Lùnastal (Scots Gaelic meaning August)
31st July - 2nd August

Pale moon doth rain, red moon doth blow.
White moon doth neither, rain or snow.

August; the start of the end of summer is here. The month of late summer which still has potential for some fierce heat and the schools going back after the long holiday. This also marks the beginning of the harvest season.

With the cutting of the first stalk of wheat, Lughnasadh arrives. Lugh, the pan-Celtic God of many things was considered a solar deity and was honoured at this time as the first grain harvest of the season and the last of the summer fruits were gathered. The festival is also named Lammas in reverence to the grain for baking bread. As well as gathering in the harvest, the focus here is centred around community, the coming together to share in the bounty of the harvest and breaking bread together. The bread harvest was vital to the ancestors as it was a staple food. They delighted and rejoiced in the success of the harvest that grew from the power raised from the festival rites at Beltane. Time now to start preserving fruits and storing the grain for the winter and at the same time, acknowledge and appreciate the effort and co-operation of the community whose hard work has paid off. Reap what you sow. The mother archetype is honoured at this festival.

This is the time in my practice to reconnect to the land where I live and to myself (getting outside barefoot), releasing and freeing what needs to go and appreciate what I have grown and how *I* have grown. It is a recognition of my abundance, and holding that in gratitude. Taking time to reflect on who I was and where I was at Imbolg and see, witness, that growth and journey, the successes and failings, overcoming of challenges and learning of lessons. It is looking forward to the full harvest moon to release that gratitude and appreciate the riches of all that I have.

Bake some bread, give thanks to the earth, finish that project you're working on, share your abundance in this time of the first harvest, be it food, love, friendship, time, etc and enjoy the last of the longer summer days/evenings.

Autumn Equinox
Mabon,
20th September - 22nd September

September blow soft, til fruits' in the loft.

September; the month of apples, (when I think of September I think of apples immediately!) but also, the autumn equinox; equal length of light and dark, the second point of (re)balance in the year as well as celebrating the second harvest. This is the harvest associated with the orchard fruits (apples!). Again an abundant harvest was crucial for winter survival in ancient times. The arrival of autumn heralds the season of the wild.

Autumn is the exhale to spring's inhale.

Do you welcome and embrace the wilds of autumn with open arms and joy or with sadness and melancholy for the summer just gone? This betwixt season, the transition season between the sizzling joy of summer and the cold dead of winter is when everything is changing and evolving; shedding and letting go, preparing for the next stage. This is a moment to pause, to breathe, assess, to enjoy the fruits of our labours, to feel the pleasure of shedding what does not belong to us and when ready, reset and balanced, move forwards into the next chapter / phase / season. This is the final festival of the Mother archetype.

It is now that you will notice that the dark half of the year is encroaching and if living in these parts will often hear "*aye, the nights are fair drawin' in*". The equinox reflects in nature the activities we are engaging in now; the prepping for winter, gathering our stores, unwinding after the hard work through spring and summer, gently beginning to relax for a bit, moving into more contemplative and protective energies and mood. It is entirely appropriate to view the equinox as a symbolic period of Thanks Giving. Giving thanks to the land, flora and fauna for all it has provided us with, thanks to the sun for nourishing our bodies in vitamin d, health and vitality, thanks to those who have helped us this year whether personally, professionally or otherwise. Celebrate and enjoy our personal harvest of achievements or milestones. These endings are but new beginnings, to be (re)born at the spring equinox.

When considering the season and the notion of balance, consider what balance means to you. Is it the age old work/life struggle for balance? Is it centred around finances, diet, hormones? Does it have more of a yin/yang connection? Is it something to aspire to or strive for? Is it the elusive standard we are supposed to attain in order to say we have arrived (insert own desirable destination here)? Is achieving "balance" possible? Is accepting where we are, finding the eye in the storm of the chaos that is life, balance enough? How do you find the balance in you? How do you address any imbalance? While the light and dark are equal here, our own sense of balance needn't be so rigid, for instance when reviewing work versus life, a 70/30 split may give you more balance than 50/50 split of the two. Be honest with yourself and know where you are right now, including the knowing of your own incarnation of light and dark (your projected self and your shadow). Both are of equal weighting and significance and require proper attention and care as they balance and steady each other.

Just as in nature, when the trees shed their leaves, this is the perfect time to acknowledge what we are letting go of as we recalibrate our inner settings. What negative emotions or patterns or people do we need to release? What has died off in the past year? Letting it go creates space for new growth and new possibilities in the coming year. Take the time to contemplate loves and losses you have enjoyed and grieved as each are valid and equally important as part of the whole cycle, season, of life. Recognise what has come to fruition in your life this past year, what seeds did you sow, nurture and grow to magnificence - not matter how small or seemingly insignificant, there is splendour in the ordinary and the efforts made.

Samhain
Samhain, pronounced "Sow-in" (Irish Gaelic),
Samhuinn, pronounced "Sa-veen" (Scots Gaelic) or
pronounced "Sam Hane" (NEVER)
31st October - 2nd November

November's sky is chill and drear,
November's leaf is red and sear.

Late October is associated with Halloween or All Hallow's Eve, followed by Hallowmas, All Hallows Day, All Saints Day on 1st November then All Souls Day on the 2nd. In times gone by, the whole affair was known in Celtic traditions as Samhain/Samhuinn. The rituals of this fire festival were respected and revered on and around the dark moon, and that wouldn't necessarily have been 31st October (because 31st October didn't exist). The darkest sky at this time of year was considered to the be the gateway into the winter months. The agricultural beasts were brought back from the summer pastures and again walked through the fires to be sained in the smoke. The animals would then be housed over winter or slaughtered for food and other needs ie the hide for leather; no part of the animal was wasted. This is the other point where the veil between the worlds was at its thinnest (Beltane being its partner), allowing our ancestors to move between their world and ours. Of course, that also meant that any malevolent spirits could also traverse the veil, hence the need to ward them off with charms such as skulls, evolving into the jack o'lantern of today originally in the form of a tumshie (turnip) or more popular now, a pumpkin. (FYI I am #teamtumshie all the way).

This is summer's end and the reign of the Cailleach dawns. An evening of tradition awaits. Samhain is a beautiful time to remember our ancestors, honouring and celebrating those who walked this path before us, keeping their memory alive. We are here today because of those who have gone before. It is also a point at which to consider who are we and where we come from. We are the living ancestors of tomorrow, how will we be remembered? Consider what the future holds and what your own legacy will be.

This is also a fun time, especially if you involve children in dooking for apples or guising. (Guising is similar to trick or treating but better – there is no trickery, but instead the kids have to earn their treat, in full costume and by performing their party piece, usually a joke or a song in exchange for sweets, monkey nuts and maybe 50p. It was 50p in my day...)

November; the betwixt month, caught between the gorgeous autumnalness (it's a word!) of October and the glittery crazy of December. Depending which calendar you follow, we are only at the half way point in the season. The cold, arse-end of Autumn is only just starting and has not yet bit, despite the many proclamations of "Winter's here" as soon as the mercury falls into single digits after sundown. It's the full embrace of late autumn, the knowing that winter is coming and we take to lighting the fire, if we are so lucky as to have one...radiators aren't quite the same...I dream of the day I have a fire and hearth again...anyway I digress...home and hearth is where it's at. And candles! Lots and lots of candles.

The chill in the air increases as the darkness deepens and the days shorten. This is the season of the witch, the time to honour the crone archetype, a transition period, of transformation, of evolution, of turning inward. It is dark and its energy contemplative, shadowy, truth seeking, quiet, nourishing and soulful. A perfect time to continue the letting go (or to finally let go) of what does not serve you any longer, and a time of awakening to what does, as well as taking this time for introspection and finding order. This is the time before the pause; I'm in my home and nesting, tending the hearth, coorying down prepping for hibernation. I look forward to this point of the year, each and every year – can you tell? You can keep your spring and summer, I'll keep my late autumn.

Winter Solstice
Yule pronounced "yool", Midwinter
20th December - 22nd December

If Christmas Day be bright and clear, there'll be two winters in the year.

December; the busiest month of the modern year! So the Wheel turns now to the winter solstice, the longest/darkest night of the year. The dying sun, being reborn again to live another cycle. This is time for reflection, gratitude, looking ahead and finding peace in the present. To fully appreciate the returning light of the sun, we need to embrace the deep, still, quietude of the darkness. From this darkness we can find our reason for joy and belonging, to celebrate with our kith and kin.

Our ancestors remain with us in the darkness, just as at Samhain, and this is a beautiful time of year to hold them in our thoughts and perhaps include mementos or significant heirlooms in our traditions or decor. This particular festival is probably the one with the most traditions associated with it, such as the evergreen tree, rich foods, the nativity, family togetherness, gift giving, and more. The cross over from

Yule to Christmas is pretty seamless in today's world as Christmas has become a more cultural and annual tradition than a religious one. The majority of those trimmings, stories and folklore are all steeped in Pagan origins, adopted, adapted and tweaked to suit the church and the consumer.

The mood of this festival is one of hope; hope for the returning sun to light the way and sustain all life, and hope for survival through the hard winter ahead. The energy is protective and focuses on connection to the community, to the land and to the local deity; the Cailleach rules the roost! This festival is one of joy and celebration, feasting and dancing, gifts and tokens exchanged for luck and prosperity, revelling in the success of the harvests, in the love of those near, and helping the sun find his strength again by lighting large bonfires (remember the sympathetic magic of the bonfire at summer solstice). The celebration continued with the rising of the sun at dawn. This was the last big feast as the food stocks had to last through the season and into the lean months of spring. So, following the merriment of the festival, the remainder of the period was to retire, rest, rise and sleep by the sun and live simply.

Do we dare, or do we have the time to make like nature and the ancestors, and rest? Can we embrace the quiet moments and the still moments and make these pauses long and restorative however small they may be?

December is all the emotions, all the activities, glitter, fun, crazy, stress, anxiety ridden, gluttony, a feast for all the sense, but Christmas is only a day. Yule, however is 12 evenings celebrating the festivities and is both joyous and nourishing.

As Winter Solstice draws closer, I begin to journey inwards, am all up in my head, feeling the draw go deep and hibernate, coorie in and shut the door on the outside stuff that's not important. I feel very protective of my truth and want to keep it hidden, private and away from others. Choosing with whom to share and spend my time, is crucial. The busy, exciting merry making of the season MUST be balanced with the quiet solitude I need to process, recharge and unwind. I am planning and visualising the festive period and the other side of the new year and what that might look like.

> *Rise up, auld wife, and shake yer feathers,*
> *Dinnae think that we are beggars,*
> *We're jist some bairns come oot tae play,*
> *Rise up and gie us oor Hogmanay*
> ~ J.C. Thomson, 1890 ~

Then back to Imbolc in roughly 6 weeks time as the cycle returns to itself to begin again.

Having seasonal markers throughout the year can help to ground yourself in the present, slow down the charge of time and the sense of time slipping away. They give something to look forward to in bite size chunks and are a way for creating traditions and rituals spread over the 12 months, rather than big blow outs a couple of times a year. Nothing lavish nor expensive is required, even at Yule! I have personal rituals that I engage in at each festival, some involve the family, for example at Halloween and at Christmas as part of my 12 nights of Yuletide, but the connection to Her and to the earth, to the sights and smells of the seasons, to checking in with myself and appreciating all that I have and all that I can give to others is what is important to me. The sense of rhythm my annual cycle has by following the seasonal wheel is comforting as I observe and connect to the changes in the natural world around me; my anchor.

Everything continually cycling and spiralling simultaneously.

Awaken Your Wild You

6

Lunar

The Moon is my compass, my clock & my calendar.
~ Lissa Corra ~

In modern, nature based spirituality, the moon features heavily, with focus on certain phases and aspects. But in times gone by, the moon wasn't revered in Celtic spirituality as much as the sun; the sun gave life and was prayed to for its return at the Winter Solstice. The moon lit a dark night and marked the passage of time through its constant cycle. It was however, enchanting. Its allure was as captivating to our ancestors as it is to us, as we gaze upon the same orb, reflecting those sun beams down to us here in the form of blessed, mystical, magical moon beams.

I have been mesmerised by the moon since childhood, staring up at it from the car window or looking out from my bedroom window. Seeing her in the sky always makes me smile and I like to greet her when I see her. The moon is a She to me. She has long been associated with grandmother energy and the Goddess, specifically Greek Celene and Roman Luna. Seeing her during the day feels like a gift. I have witnessed some spectacular sights particularly when she has been low and full and LARGE known as perigee (SUPERmoon when the moon is closest to the earth) as opposed to apogee (micromoon when the moon is furthest from the earth). Neither of these terms however has anything to do with turning young boys into white rabbits...but if you want to try it...here's the incantation :

> *"filigree, apogee, pedigree, perigee!"*
> *~ Miss Eglentine Price, Bedknobs & Broomsticks ~*

The most frustrating thing about moon gazing is that the sheer beauty I see and awe I feel can never, ever be captured on camera. It used to annoy me that every time I took a photo it was nothing other than a blur on screen that looked like I'd smeared the lens. Now (that I don't take her photo) I appreciate her in that moment and all the emotions that I experience are purely for that specific point in time. It is a pause, a breath, pure joy and a treasured memory. That's all it can ever be and is as it ought to be.

    She is always present even when we can't see her; controlling the tides and weather. Her energetic pull is strong and powerful. Even Greek Physician, Hippocrates of Kos, who is regarded as the father of modern medicine, says so as he wrote in the fifth century B.C. :

> *"one who is seized with terror, fright and madness during the night is being visited by the goddess of the moon."*

Madness and insanity was thought to be have been caused by the moon, which is where the word lunatic and the condition lunacy come from:

"Lunatic is an antiquated term referring to a person who is seen as mentally ill, dangerous, foolish, or crazy – conditions once attributed to "lunacy". The word derives from lunaticus meaning "of the moon" or "moonstruck". The term originally referred mainly to epilepsy and madness, as diseases thought to be caused by the moon."
Wikipedia

Fun Fact: Did you know that pregnancy used to be calculated by the lunar cycles rather than menstrual cycles as is today? (You never know when this will come up in a pub quiz!)

To measure time by the lunar cycle you need to know the phases of the cycle and how long they last. A full lunation from New Moon to Dark Moon is approximately 29.5 days long. The moon cycles through several phases each with a different energy connected to it. A full lunar year is 13 moons long but does not always fit with the Gregorian or the Ogham calendars. Trying to make them fit in the same time frame will only hurt your head. Don't try, it's not the *Krypton Factor*! 13 full moons do manage to make it into the 365 days some years but not 13 full lunar months.

These moon cycles each have many faces, phases, seasons and energies depending on where she is in her cycle, mirroring earth and woman. Each phase also has its own energy, emotions, meaning and attachments *to you*. Learn to follow your intuition and be guided by your own connection too, not just the suggested prescription below.

Moon Phases

New
The first teeny, tiny slice of the waxing crescent as it is glimpsed in the sky. Also known as the Witches New Moon.

This is the the business end of manifesting, intention setting for the coming cycle and starting over, for renewal. Time to start new projects and accept new opportunities. Make sure to view the new skelf-like sliver outdoors without any obstruction or filter as it is bad luck to look upon it through a window!

New Moon Activities:
- Draw your tarot cards for the coming cycle and use them to help set your intentions.
- Set out any crystals you use, on your window sill to absorb the lunar energy.
- Set intentions for goals that you want to achieve this cycle as well as longer term ones.
- Work a spell for manifesting or to draw in good fortune.
- Plant seeds in the garden or in pots.
- Have your hair cut.
- Take a ritual bath to cleanse yourself prior to working your ritual.
- Meditate and do a full body scan to identify any pain or niggles and set to resolve them.
- Gather in a Women's Circle.

Waxing Crescent
The crescent shape with the horns pointing to the left like a backwards 'C'. This is the point at which you will be able to identify potential obstacles to your plans and work out the solutions. The energy in this phase is that of the Maiden, it's exciting and fresh, the air is ripe with possibility.

First Quarter
The half moon, like a D in the sky. Creativity is flowing. It's lunar spring time and the time is now for taking action as momentum is gaining and growing. The energy is rising.

Waxing Gibbous
This Maiden phase is evolving into the Mother phase. A period of continued growth, development and expansion. Refine your plans and actions to achieve desired results. Exercise some patience too.

Full
The moon is full and round. It is the most potent and powerful phase, perfect to birth something new with confidence or to literally give birth. This phase represents the Mother archetype. It's lunar summer time and all is in full bloom. This is the time to expect results from that which you have been working on as well as to cleanse, purge and purify yourself or your space or project with the clarity of her luminescent grace.

Full Moon Activities:
- Laying out any crystals or jewellery (especially silver) that you work with or wear regularly, on your windowsill over night to be charged by the energy of the Moon.
- Make Moon Water by placing a suitable container, with an open top (I use a silver quaiche), filled with water either on the window sill or in your garden, overnight and in the morning you will have Moon charged water to use in magical working or to water your plants or add to your morning tea/coffee.
- Read your tarot cards to check in on your progress so far and for the coming 2 weeks.
- Review where you are in your plans with the

intentions you set at the New Moon.
- Moon bathe - just like sun bathing but at night and most probably in warmer clothing(!) but lying out under the moon and relax/meditate.
- Meditation.
- Gather the women and Circle.
- Light a candle and switch off the electronics for a slow, soft, even romantic evening.
- Sleep with the curtains/blinds open.
- Embrace the Full Moon energy and vitality, your inner Goddess and enjoy yourself (with your partner or solo).
- Use your menstrual blood (ideally fresh but if not, freeze it when you're bleeding and defrost it in a little water - if you don't freeze it will STINK! Like raw meat gone bad.....blergh..) mixed in with the charged moon water to feed your houseplants or garden, create art whether painting with the blood or mixing it into glue or paint to charge your creation with your very essence, anoint yourself with a spot or smear of blood to honour you and your sovereignty with Grandmother Moon as your witness.
- Dance, shake it all loose, release everything no longer serving you. This is one practice I 100% recommend!

Waning Gibbous
This is the best time for letting go, releasing and banishing and breaking bad habits. Time too for gratitude and giving thanks for your blessings, work and endeavours the came to fruition at the full phase.

Third/Last Quarter
The moon hangs in the sky like a backwards 'D'. This is the time to learn from your mistakes and make any changes to your situation. It is also perfect time for going inwards to

face the many shadows lurking. Why do you do what you do? Why don't you do what you want to do? What are your true values? How and where have you grown? What are your triggers? Why do they trigger you so? Who do you want to be versus who you are? It's lunar autumn, make like the trees and start shedding.

Waning Crescent
She takes on the appearance of the letter C as the horns point to the right. This is the surrender into the end of the cycle with the wisdoms gained from the cycle and now you reach the point of assessment. Listen to your intuition, seek out forgiveness; either from yourself or from/for that of another.

Dark
The moon is in her darkest phase, hidden completely from sight in the void between waning and waxing. Cycle complete but not yet begun again. This is the pause, the reset, the recognition for your accomplishments. It's lunar winter and the moon of the Crone. The Dark moon and the New moon are often used interchangeably by the majority of people and all the printed or online calendars, but they are different. The Dark Moon is the period where the moon is 100% invisible, moving into the New Moon phase only with that first tiny slither of crescent gently glowing through the inky depths of space. For the moon descends to her lowest ebb, hidden and hibernating in the winter of her cycle, greeting the death of the last cycle and awaiting the rebirth of the next.

Dark Moon Activities :
- Rest. Take a pause before starting over.
- Take a pause to reflect on the cycle just gone. Exhaling to release all. A contented sigh relaxing and

recognising the end.
- Take a moment to gather yourself, nourish yourself, be by yourself before facing the world again, renewed and ready to begin the next cycle.
- Draw an oracle card for the cycle just gone and another for the one to come.
- Drink in the contemplative, inward, soulful energy of the dark, along side your cuppa.

New again to continue the cycle.

If working with the moon is new to you these are just some ideas to get to going or perhaps give you an opportunity to change up what you usually do. I used to have set rituals that I worked with and carried out each and every Dark, New and Full Moon but these days I go with however I am feeling that day, sometimes just looking up at the Moon and spending a couple of minutes in her presence is enough and other times it is a good couples of hours deep in ritual and sacred work. You will find what works best for you, and each cycle may vary or be the same. Go with your own flow.

Names of Moons

Just as each phase of the moon has corresponding meanings and energies, so does each individual moon cycle each month. Again, there are no set rules that in a specific month you need to be working with that particular energy or focus on that particular activity. I prefer to tailor the meaning to the season and to what's happening in my life rather than prescribed thematics of each lunation.

Month	Celtic Ogham	Old English	Native American	Other
January	Rowan: Moon of Perseverance	Old Moon	Wolf Moon	Ice Moon or Moon after Yule.
February	Ash: Moon of Journeying	Wolf Moon	Snow Moon	Hunger or Storm Moon
March	Alder: Moon of Balance & Rebirth	Lenten Moon	Worm Moon	Chaste or Crow or Sap Moon
April	Willow: Moon of Healing	Egg Moon	Pink Moon	Waking or Hare or Fish Moon
May	Hawthorn: Moon of Fertility	Milk Moon	Flower Moon	Corn Moon
June	Oak: Moon of Strength	Flower Moon	Strawberry Moon	Planting or Honey or Rose Moon
July	Holly: Moon of Encirclement	Hay Moon	Buck Moon	Thunder Moon
August	Hazel: Moon of Wisdom	Grain Moon	Sturgeon Moon	Lightening or Fruit Moon
September	Vine: Moon of Harvest	Corn Moon	Harvest Moon	Barley Moon
October	Ivy: Moon of Storms & Protection	Harvest Moon	Hunter Moon	Blood Moon
November	Reed: Moon of the Hearth	Hunters Moon	Beaver Moon	Frost or Mourning Moon
December	Elder: Moon of Endings	Oak Moon	Cold Moon	Long nights Moon
	Birch: Moon of New Beginnings			

The other cycle the moon journeys through is the zodiac. She moves through each of the 12 (or is it now 13?) zodiac signs with every cycle, spending roughly 2.5 days in each sign. Which ever sign she is in at the dark moon phase will be in the exact opposite sign come full moon. Again the signs have their own associated meanings, energies and correspondences and they are further specified to you as an individual person depending upon how the planets and stars were placed at the exact time of your birth. You can get this information, called your natal chart, on line, which will give you your specific information and how you can then work with and relate to the moon and the zodiac cycle. My star sign, known as the sun sign is Gemini, my moon sign is Libra and my rising sign is Leo; 2 air and 1 fire sign, but do you want to know something? Confession time; I no longer use the zodiac for anything...yes I am a "typical" Gemini, but I don't pay attention to or connect with it any more! It doesn't feature in my practice. That may change again in the future (I am a Gemini afterall...) but for me at this time, it simply no longer enriches my practice or connection. Despite the fact I recently reread my natal chart and it remains ridiculously accurate. Astrology just isn't working for me right now and I don't need it. So many cycles so many layers.

Are you tuned to the moon?

7

Menstrual

We are women and we are bloody magnificent. Yes we are!
~ Lissa Corra ~

This is one of those topics the finally is becoming less and less taboo as more women embrace the art of honest conversation without shame or, more probably, embarrassment.

Are you all at sea with your moods and energy levels, struggling to keep all the plates spinning and every day life on a constant even keel? Want to know a secret? That's not how your body is set up to function! This chapter will reveal to you the secrets and mysteries of your womb space, that inner cauldron of power and your internal calendar, learning how to track and chart your cycle. Discover why this is essential work. Menstrual wisdom is for all women, from girls just about to begin their cycling journey, teens, women in their 20's, 30's 40's, 50's, 60's and beyond, for the peri and post menopausal and for women who use hormone contraception or HRT - you still cycle and have ebbs and flows! We are not linear beings, but cyclic beings striving to exist in a man-made linear world.

As a 43 year old perimenopausal woman, I have lived with and tolerated my menstruations for many a cycle (almost 30 years...WTF?). That was until I was 38 or 39 years old and learned about my cycle. Not just the days I'm "on" but the whole cycle from start to finish to start again. And can I just say, "Woah!" Why are we not taught about that in school when we get our leaflet and are shown tampons by the school nurse? Since my discovery I have completely changed my perception around my own cycle. I actually look forward to my bleed time now rather than the irritated tolerance I used to regard it with. That last sentence may seem a bit "out there" for many people, but yes, I look forward to it because I understand it; my cycle, our cycles as women. Mind, we are not linear beings but cyclical, continuously revolving each and every month.

Our cycle is not purely one of bleeding and not bleeding. There is so much more to it, and to us, than that. The days in-between our period are just as important to how we function and live, as the period itself. We don't just coast long for 3 weeks then BAM! bleeding for a few days and then back to "normal". You may notice that you feel a little more tired, less patient, or freaking awesome and alive at different points in your cycle, yet be completely unaware that this is *because* of your cycle you are feeling like this. Who knew this already? I know I certainly didn't until I began charting my cycle **daily**. It is an exercise I heartily recommend, as it opened my eyes to the patterns in my own life. Tracking my cycle has been the biggest and best gift I have given to myself and the most valuable lesson I have learned in how to care for and work with my physical and mental health. I'm not exaggerating! By consciously monitoring my ebbs and flows, moods, energy levels, primal need for chocolate and the release that only really good/creative swearing brings, I have seen where I am full of life, motivation and actually achieving the tasks on my to-do list compared to when I get very little done because I need to chill out and coorie in. Remember I mentioned that we are cyclical not linear? (I am going to keep bringing this up because it's important!) This is the reason why I was getting so frustrated with my bullet journal (which I no longer use) and why in some weeks, most of my tasks were being carried over into another week, not even just carried over onto the next day, I needed a whole other week to catch up!

Make friends with your menstrual cycle. It's not as bat-shit crazy as it sounds! It will revolutionise your life. Menstrual Cycle Awareness (an expression created by *Red School* co-founders, Alexandra Pope and Sjanie Hugo Wurlitzer) is the foundation to our physical and mental health and well being, it is our innate connection to ourselves at our very core. Knowing your own body and understanding when something isn't quite right puts the power and control back in your own hands.

Since I had my first ever period, I have recorded it on either my calendar or in my diary; always tracking when I was "due on" but never gave the other 21 days in-between a second thought. The cycle was 28 days, give or take, with a week each month to bleed and rage and weep and eat and legitimately be allowed to be thoroughly pissed off for no good reason. When I was working as a Senior Manager with 5 men (around 16 years ago), they actually knew when it was my time of the month and had it on the calendar in the Boss's office - I shit you not. They tended to stay clear at that time as I was "crabbit". Even now, I'm still uncertain as how how I feel about that, despite uncomfortably laughing it off at the time.

We flow through the phases of birth, growth, harvest and decay before returning to rebirth again in our cycle of life, and our menstrual cycle is no different. We move in cycles, our bodies revolve through a full cycle and range of hormonal changes every single month (unless the cycle has been stopped or over ridden by means such as pregnancy, hormonal contraception, HRT, chemotherapy etc). We have distinct energies at each of the phases, specific needs and experience varying emotions that affect our moods, appetite, sleep patterns, creativity, esteem, sex drive and more. Every month! **Cyclical!! Not linear!! Very important!!** What we feel or experience at the time of menstruation is the polar opposite to when we are ovulating, for instance. Even post menopausally, we still cycle, even though we don't have a monthly bleed, the body doesn't reprogramme to a linear state.

Understanding that we have a continuously revolving cycle will aid you in planning and living your life to suit your needs. If you can imagine that your menstrual cycle is divided into 4 seasons, just like the year; Winter, Spring, Summer, Autumn, or the phases of the Moon; Dark Moon, First Quarter/Waxing, Full Moon, Third Quarter/Waning. Each phase or season represents a specific part of the cycle your body is working through during that week, with its associated effects and needs. Depending upon whether you are cycling "naturally" or say, are on the pill, pregnant or post menopause, will determine *how* you track your cycle. If you do not bleed any longer or you do not have an organic cycle you can track the cycle of the moon as its lunation is 29.5 days (NOT 28!) and follows the same pattern of increasing and decreasing energies

Let's look at the each season and phase in turn:

Winter

Days 1-7 of your cycle, also known as the dark moon phase, menstruation. Its energy is the estrogen producing, feminine yin. The archetype is the Crone. This is recorded from the first day of your proper bleed, not the pre-period spotting. It is a time to be reflective, withdrawn (anti-social even), passive, to hibernate, focus on rest, self care, food (including chocolate), bubble baths and plenty tea. Not exactly cracking on with all that roller skating in skin tight trousers and partying that the tampon adverts want us to be doing. That comes later.

Spring

Days 8-14, the waxing moon phase, pre-ovulation. It is still in the estrogen producing phase but the energy is masculine, yang. The archetype here is the Maiden. This phase follows the symbolic death of winter, when we come back up for air, after hibernating. This is all about new and fresh ideas, new beginnings, the rebirth, full of hope, dynamism and enthusiasm. Beware however, although this is *pre*-ovulation, if you are looking to get pregnant, days 10-15 are generally HOT! (this is due to sperm being able to live in the fallopian tubes for up to seven days after sex, meaning it's ready and waiting for that egg to be released at ovulation).

Summer

Days 15-21, the full moon phase, ovulation. Remaining masculine in yang energy, now producing progesterone. The archetype is the Mother. Remember the scene from *Pretty*

Woman when Kit was encouraging Vivian as she approaches Edward's car? "Work it, work it baby, own it". YAS! This is you right now! In your A Game! You are at your peak, your optimum, getting shit done! This is a very expressive and social time. Get those white jeans and roller blades on and get going. While the phase lasts a week, it is worth noting that actual ovulation is a very short timescale (once the egg is released it can only survive 12-24 hours unless fertilised), which coincidentally matches that of the British summer time, blink and you miss it!

Autumn

Days 22-28, the waning moon phase, pre-menstrual. Feminine yin energy returning, still producing progesterone. The archetype is the wild, wise woman. This is time to store reserves of energy, take stock of the previous month, winding down readying for winter. If you suffer, then this is PMS central with the cramps (try raspberry leaf tea. I drank it by the bucket load when I was still pregnant twelve days over my due date, but it is ace for period cramps too). Your emotions may be temperamental, fragile, swinging back and forth and tears may be more readily available. And do you know what? It's allowed. It's yours to feel so give permission to yourself to feel all the feels, because they are yours. Own them.

*Disclaimer - I am not a Dr and my findings have been based purely on my own personal experiences and upon the research I have conducted myself. Not everyone will have a 28 cycle. Cycles ranging from 24-35 days are equally "normal".

I have been tracking my cycle in this manner for over 4 years now and I noticed very clearly that my seasons didn't fit neatly into the 7 day boxes as described above. MY own personal seasonal cycles look more like the following:

Spring - Days 4/5 - Day 10 (Lots of energy and in a generally good mood with plenty of creative juices flowing)
Summer - Day 11 - Day 18 (I am a Goddess and am getting all the things done!)
Autumn - Day 19 - Days 25/26 (My tolerance levels are waning faster than the moon. Around day 25/26, I'd rather you didn't speak to me)
Winter - Day 26/27 - Day 3/4 (From day 26 I CRAVE solitude and tend to keep my diary as free as much as is possible).

So how does all this fit in with modern living? It is not exactly practical to take time off from family/work for 3 days every 4 weeks to menstruate. Have you read *The Red Tent* by Anita Diamant? The women, whose cycles are all in sync both with each others and with the phases of the moon, bug out together in the Red Tent for 3 days, no men, just a sacred space for themselves and each other at the new moon, to bleed. It is reported too that in Native American tribes, women went to the Moon Lodge at their moon time and they were revered for their power. This all sounds pretty amazing if you ask me, but anyway, today we don't have time for a wee 3 day holiday. We have busy lives and careers and families that we need to get on with, not taking that sacred time out to rest, nourish and gather. We pretend we are linear and we rely on paracetamol. I am no different in that respect; a busy mum with a full time schedule, but I did implement some changes, such as ensuring I don't plan anything outwith the necessary in my winter week and up the number of bubble baths. The dishes will not always be done, the clean laundry not put away and the general state of the house becomes just that: a state. BUT when that phase moves onto the next, everything is caught up with again and more. It's all about balance and listening to my body. Slowing down when I need rest, going for it when my energy spikes and planning according to the flexibility I have.

I think if we are honest, menstruation is all hushed up and still referred to, by some, as "women's stuff", because in the past, that is how we were taught about it. I remember being in Primary 7 (so 11 years old) and having the talk with the nurse. All the girls in our year were in the classroom and the boys were all sent out to play football for the duration. They had no idea what we were being told, truth be told, in hindsight neither did we; plain facts of body function followed by a selection of pads and tampons to look at and a pamphlet to read. And there in lies the problem - excluding the boys, and relying solely on the facts about what happens only at the time of your period, rather than looking at the cycle as a whole and all it encompasses. If they (and we) knew what we were dealing with, perhaps then there would be far less ignorance around the subject. In particular, a greater understanding from the male species with regards the mood swings and emotional peaks and troughs experienced by their mothers, sisters, friends, girlfriends or wives. Too many men, and to be fair, many women too, completely disrespect women with judgmental and ignorant comments such as "she's emotional / hysterical / bitchy / insert any other [in]appropriate name". It would be helpful for those holding such beliefs to understand that feelings are not wrong or inconvenient, they are a barometer of how you are experiencing something at any given moment. To experience emotions is human, to acknowledge them is a strength not a weakness. Also, it's worth noting that as our emotions are heightened around the time of our period, so too is our bullshit detector

Big : "Don't be a bitch"
Carrie : "I'm not. I'm just being myself"
~ Sex and the City ~

Climbing back down from my soapbox, I say let us connect to and understand our own cycles, celebrate the wonderment of them and what they mean to each of us. Let us reclaim our cycles and teach the young women today the power of their cycles, to empower themselves in owning, loving and appreciating their bodies and autonomy.

So, how do you track where you are in your cycle and plan for the weeks ahead? There are many apps available for you to download which will keep you on track. I can't recommend any of them as I don't and have never used any of them. I'm analogue when it comes to tracking, I need paper and pencils! The most popular method and the one I use is with a mandala. The mandala is basically a pie chart split into 28 wedges (you can adjust the number of wedges to the length of your own cycle), each individual wedge represents one day. I find this works most effectively because it is easy to see at a glance where I am, and by using colour it is even easier to identify where I am and when. Also you can track more than just your cycle pattern, for instance I track my sleep (the amount I get), my mood on each day, actual days of bleeding and the spotting, changes in cervical fluid (very important to know when you are fertile!), energy levels, feelings and sensations in my body and more.

You may now be thinking, what does this magical mandala look like? There are plenty you can down load and print off but I prefer to draw mine out each month as I can tweak it to suit my needs. I used to have a dedicated journal for menstrual tracking, just page after page of mandalas, which worked great for me for the past 3 years but more recently I have just drawn it onto a piece of A5 paper and stapled it into my daily journal.

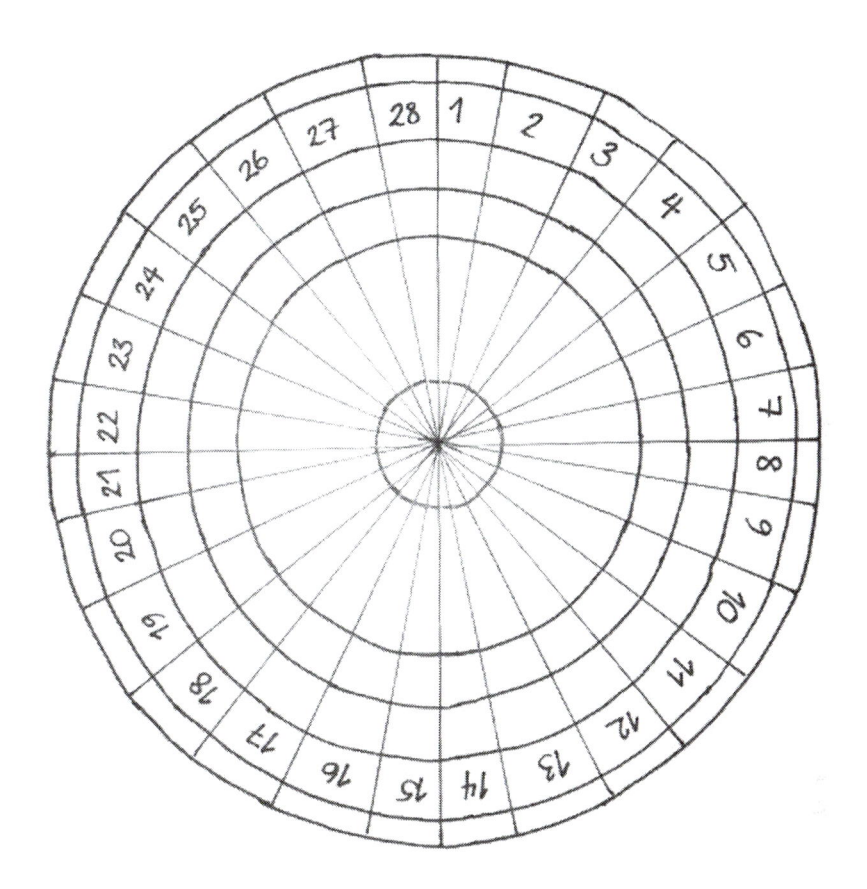

With the mandalas you can get as creative and fancy or keep as plain as you like. It's your own calendar to use so make it work for you. I like to colour code my weeks around the outside ~ blue for winter, green for spring, red for summer and purple for autumn ~ and in the centre I block in the full colour the days I am bleeding (red) and use dots for the spotting or lighter days. I also highlight in the centre, in yellow, the days I am ovulating, which I can tell by the cervical fluid I am producing at that time (FYI it's when it resembles the consistency of uncooked egg white). The other rows I have marked out are for the day of my cycle, below that it's the date, then the number of hours of sleep or if I am tracking something else that month. The larger space is for notes on feelings, mood, cramps or anything I think is relevant. Some people like to mark in the lunar phases and astrological signs too, I tried that in the past but it didn't add anything to my experience or how the month was going so ditched it. The beauty of the mandala method is that you can track what ever you want and try new things, chop and change to see what does and doesn't work for you.

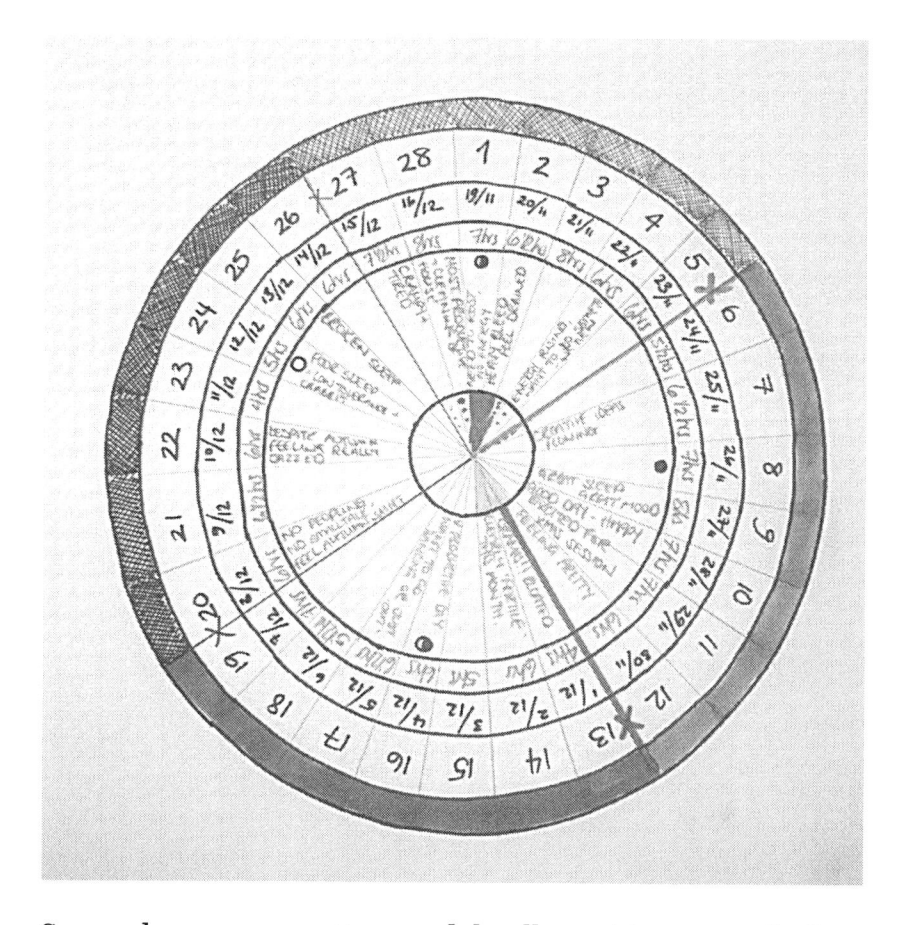

So you have your pretty mandala all good to go, marked up with the days of your cycle and the dates, but how do you know when you are moving into spring or summer or are in your autumn or winter weeks? We have been so used to living with only one or two notions of a sort of cycle, PMS and bleeding, that it can take a bit of time and practice to tune into our own bodies again. With daily charting of moods and energy or even just sleep you'll start to see and feel the shifts. My husband can also tell my seasons now especially when I come out of winter as my mood is so much lighter and am generally full of chat, or as he says "so, you're now on the up swing" where as the previous few days I'm quiet and reserved giving off very definite "do not disturb" vibes. Spring week usually means a lift in mood, a need to get going and take action again, imagine and create new ideas, feeling joy and laughing more, rising energy and sex drive, an all round sense of fun and good humour. Moving into summer I tend to recognise the shift, not just physically from the aforementioned cervical fluid, but in my confidence, in the condition of my hair, a reduction in the amount of sleep I need to feel good (compared to late autumn and winter), not wanting stodgy or heavy foods, wanting to be with people and socialising more. Then the shift into autumn when I want to people less and I feel my tolerance hit the down slope, the honesty is flowing hence forth and forth with from my mouth. I'm more emotionally and physically sensitive and prickly, and I start to feel bloated around my middle. I also find that my notion for a wee glass of red in the evenings is more pronounced. The sure fire way I know I have shifted into winter is when I get the unequivocal and sudden feeling of "I need to be alone, people be gone!". It lands with a thud and is most resolute. I don't want to be around or converse with anyone! In the book *Wild Power* by Alexandra Pope and Sjanie Hugo Wurlitzer, this is called the Separation Chamber. This feeling heralds my arrival into my inner winter.

This revelation didn't happen in one cycle however, identifying the transition from one season/phase into the next took months. I started by following the pattern Days 1-7 are winter, 8-14 are spring, 15-21 are summer then 22-28 are autumn until I found my own rhythm and pattern which doesn't neatly fit into a 7 day equal spread necessarily. Some months I have a longer autumn or a shorter spring. Acknowledging and listening to my body and my cycle are a huge part of my self care practice and my acknowledgement that Days 25/26 are good for other people's self care too...unless direct truths are wanted...

After a few months of using mandalas (a new one for each cycle, beginning on Day 1) you can easily identify patterns of behaviour, like when you need more sleep, when is the best time to exercise or have busy days for catching up with friends or schedule meetings or are at peak fertility. It is also apparent when things go off kilter and your cycle changes (for me that is happening presently with the onset of perimenopause, my cycle varies between 24 and 31 days, once I get to Day 24 I'm just waiting for the sign that I am about to start.)

There are 2 stand out patterns I noticed since tracking which are :

1. I cramp worse when ovulating that I do when premenstrual! SHOCKER! This blew my mind.
2. You know how there is this stereotypical nesting period just before a woman gives birth, where she has an almost primal need to get her house in order before just before she goes into labour? Well, turns out that's what I do just before I bleed! The most obvious indicator to me that I am going to start my period the next day is when I want and need to clean the house, with the sheer vigour and vim of a woman possessed.

I find the combination of tracking my cycle as above coupled with my daily journalling to be an invaluable tool in my self care kit, and the most vital. I have been able to better plan and schedule and live my life which has been revolutionary both for me and my family! For years, ie from ages 14 to 39, I used to mark off on the calendar the week I was "due on" and nothing more. I was never aware of what it meant to be a cyclic woman and what that involved.

Understanding now what it means to cycle and experience the changes in hormones and energy levels and fluctuating weight levels over the course of each month has opened my eyes to a whole new world and it is empowering to stand here as a sovereign woman knowing how my body works and why. I just wish I knew abut it earlier, but better late than never.

This is the stuff we need to reclaim and teach to our daughters and girlfriends, and mothers too who are possibly post menopausal, well into the crone years and have never known what it is like to live in sync with their own bodies which may have been medically managed - I'm looking at you, my family GP who put me on the pill at 16 to "regulate" my periods!

If you don't currently track your entire monthly cycle, please give it a go. I'd love to hear how you get on after a couple of months, or if you do track, tell me, what has been your biggest lesson or revelation?

In my own menstrual learning journey, I have found the work of Lisa Lister, Alexandra Pope & Sjanie Hugo Wurlitzer invaluable. More recently I would also offer up the fantastic work of Berrion Berry, Maisie Hill, Claire Baker and Talitha Joy as wise menstrual educators. These women are all on the normal social media platforms and have their work published in books and podcasts that ought to be on the reading and listening lists for all women! (in my humble opinion.)

Another popular way to track our menstrual cycle, particularly over the past 5 years or so, has been to align your cycle with the moon. I have to honest right here and state that this is not something I subscribe to. If you do and find a connection, then great, but it is not for me, and I'll explain why.

The myth tells that women's menstrual cycles are governed by the lunar cycle. Yes, the moon controls the earth's waters and we are made up of about 60% water (I actually though it was 70% but a quick google search told me different). Yes, our menstrual cycles are cyclic and the phases of our cycles can be described in the same manner as the moon's. The associated energy of the moon's effect on earth is reflected in our moods and own energy levels, BUT there endeth the story. The tales that tell how all women in ancient times bled together under the dark and new moon, then ovulated under the full, are unfounded. They are lovely stories and it would be beautiful if true. I mean, that's exactly how it would have happened some of the time but not all the time, not every month. It makes sense to live in harmony with the natural world in a time and place before electric light, modern medicine and endocrine disruptors but having your period be in sync with the moon is simply another stick with which to bash us with, another standard we're to aspire to and meet or feel inadequate when we fail.

Unless your own cycle is 29.5 days long every month, you won't ever be "in sync" with the moon, menstrually. Let's take my cycle for instance, this month I am bleeding on/with the dark moon. I haven't done this for almost a year. Last month I started 3 days after the new moon. For most of the this year I have been bleeding either side of the full moon, but have actually travelled through and bled with all phases. Why? Because my own cycle varies each month and ranges between 27-31 days long and the other month it was only 24 days! I'm not a robot. Here's the thing - your body IS in sync...with itself! The only time your cycle isn't "in sync" with your own natural rhythms, ebbs and flows of your ovaries is when you are taking the contraceptive pill (or have the injection or implant) which suppresses your cycle, or when you are pregnant or are undergoing medical treatment such as chemotherapy. At these times it maybe useful or beneficial to follow the lunar cycle but when we are following our own cycle please know that you are in sync with your own body and that's who you're supposed to be in sync with!

This whole red moon or white moon bleeding with particular phases of the moon is something that at one time I bought into it too! However, I'm sick to my ovaries of this New Age expectation of how to and when we are supposed to menstruate. The lunar energy is powerful. I can feel it, but it doesn't mean that I ignore my own inner energy and being; self first, lunar second. This month I am aligned (not synced) with the dark moon and my own moods are deep rooted in need to rest, in solitude, pretty much hibernate, my inner winter phase, in the same way the moon does when it is invisible in the night's sky. It won't be next month and that's how it goes.

Am I tuned to the moon? Absofuckinglutely! I love the moon and how it's connected to our planet and her energy and beauty. Is my menstrual cycle? Nope! It's my period and I'll bleed when I need to.

8

Life

Tell me, what is it you plan to do with your one wild and precious life?
~ Mary Oliver ~

Birth. Life. Death. If we are lucky, we are born, live a full and happy life into old age and pass away peacefully in our sleep enveloped in the love of our dearest ones. Then, if we believe it to be the case, we are reborn again to live another cycle on the earthly plane. So on and so forth. But this *life* bit in the middle, what's that all about?

Dr Jonas Frisen, a Swedish stem cell biologist, discovered that the body renews itself in its entirety every 7-10 years, which handily coincides with the different stages and milestones we reach as we age, each phase taking roughly two spins of the seven year cycles. By applying his finding to a woman's life cycle I find it looks like this :

- birth to puberty = 00 to 14 years old (approx)
- puberty (maiden) to mother = 14 to 28 years of age
- mother to matriarch = 28 to 42 years of age
- matriarch to crone (elder) = 42 to 63 years of age
- crone until death = around 63 years onwards until the last breath is drawn. With good luck, health and genes, this will be the longest of the phases lasting two, three, four or maybe even five or six cycles more.

As we travel along the path of life, the journey leads us through cycles and phases. We all face a life's journey; childhood, maiden, mother, matriarch (wild woman), crone (wise woman), returning to the great mother, and if you are so inclined, rinse and repeat. But we won't journey the same route or meet each phase at the same time or in the same order. In fact you may not subscribe to this journey or recognise these archetypes at all, but if you come along with me for now, there is much to be unravelled, reclaimed and revered as we evolve and transform through each phase embracing the lessons we have learned from the previous phase. To understand and consider these phases in more detail, let's look at them.

Maiden

What does that word mean to you? What image immediately springs to mind? All it means is an unmarried girl or young woman, and sometimes an older unmarried woman; a spinster. It can, perhaps, seem like an old fashioned word. The images I automatically think of are of fair maidens of Ye Olde England in the style of Maid Marian from the Robin Hood tales. Perhaps you hear maiden and think of a ship's Maiden Voyage or a newly appointed MP's Maiden Speech in parliament?

What I am referring to with the word "Maiden" is the first phase of a woman's life when she transitions from girl to young woman. It begins with Menarche, (pronounced men-*ar*-kee) her first bleed, and commences around 12 years old, give or take a year or two (I was 14 years old at the time of my Menarche, although that was not what I called it. I had never even heard it referred to as such until only a few years ago). This is the start of her journey through the cycles; not only monthly but through the rest of her life, moving through the seasons of each from Maiden to Elder.

The word maiden is synonymous with virgin. The old fashioned status of a girl's purity, her virginity, was known as her maidenhead which was her most prized possession for her husband-to-be. But the true meaning of virgin had nothing to do with her sexual status. The original meaning of virgin was an unwed woman, a sovereign woman of her own means, who made her own choices. Many a virgin had many a lover. However, with the rise of Christianity it was reframed and virgin became synonymous with chaste and purity.

Chastity, not sovereignty, became sacred.

While we are taking about language, let's consider how unmarried older women were referred to until fairly recently (not sure anyone under 75 still uses this term, but am prepared to be corrected on this point). I'm talking about the Spinster. The tone used when referring to a woman as a spinster is not particularly positive, perhaps with a shot of pity or confusion, why would anyone *choose* to be a spinster? Well, this is why: a spinster was an occupation that women held as it was a job that required skill and dexterity yet was considered beneath that of a man. During the medieval period the demand for fabric was such that spinning work was vital and a skilled spinster could earn a nice wage on her own merit. She was a woman of her own means and didn't rely upon a spouse or father in order to live. The term spinster was reference to her economic status rather than her marital one. A spinster was sovereign. May I suggest that we reclaim these titles with the dignity and sovereignty they command rather than with disdain or judgement or viewed from the patriarchal, religious standard of sacred?

Back to why am I talking about Maidens in the first place; in today's world, in patriarchal society, this is the phase of a woman's life where she is most valued for her youth and beauty. A woman's worth is determined, for the masses for the past few thousand years, from the dominant perspective; by men. The young Maiden is the prize, the trophy wife. She makes older men feel youthful, powerful and virile, and if desired, likely to easily produce an heir. Socially, it is perfectly acceptable for an older man to have a much younger wife or partner, when the reverse is much less so. Yet this is when she is least prepared for life with more naivety than experience. We need to redress this balance.

How do we do this? By acknowledging the importance of Menarche, what being a Maiden means to the individual young woman AND her mother (or primary female care giver), what we can learn from her and what we can teach her, as well as the tools/skills we can can equip her with as she walks her path to fully realising the wonderful woman she is, celebrating this rite of passage and honouring her blood rite. Empowerment and sovereignty begins with connecting to and understanding the importance of body autonomy, of mind and of soul. We do all this collectively in the village, the community, the Circle, the Red Tent.

Take a minute to think back to when you had your first period. Were you prepared beyond the basic biological chat from your mum or big sister or school nurse? How did you feel - embarrassed, ashamed, confused, ill, empowered, proud, "like a grown up"? Looking back, is there anything you would wish had gone differently? Hold on to that thought for a bit longer - we're going to come back to it later.

Let us now look a bit deeper at this Maiden. As girls, we transition in to the Maiden phase of life from around the age of 12, and it lasts until around age 28/29, when we then transition again, this time into the Mother phase. Regardless of whether we have birthed or will go on to have children is irrelevant, as women we all cycle through the each of the phases, experiencing the shifts in energies and our purpose. Some women will have an overlap of the two phases when they birth their children in their teen years or twenties, and that is their journey and their experience; both Maiden and Mother, flowing between the two interchangeably.

This Maiden time period is the season of spring, the waxing crescent moon phase and pre-ovulation. It is this springtime energy the Maiden is exerting that makes her attractive and magnetic. She is beautiful, youthful, energetic, confident and ambitious. She is a visionary. This is a time for immense growth, but also for facing the shadow side to all this exuberance; naivety and the desire to be independent and free without consideration of consequences or the wisdom of hindsight. In efforts to make it on her own, this is the time when mistakes are made (some small, some not) and lessons are learned (some the hard way), generally without the framework of strong, trusted support in the right places. This is the time of contradictions of epic proportions, which may be utterly confusing, without that support.

What is this support I am referring to? The support of women, trusted women who can share the knowledge and wisdom of the blood mysteries, the strength and power that comes from knowing and understanding our cycles, how to care for our (physical and mental) health properly. It is a trusted support network of mothers, grandmothers, older sisters, friends and aunties that will guide, be a sounding board when she's second guessing herself, helping her to navigate the tricky waters of dating and relationships, of situations she is uncomfortable with, and be there without judgement to catch her when she falls. Which she will; we all do. It's knowing she has someone when she is in need of help. This is what is missing today. Not everyone is lucky enough to have that sort of relationship with their mum, they may not have a relationship at all with their mum for any number of reasons, and so the circle is the support.

The Red Tents and Moon Lodges of yesteryear were destroyed and outlawed. The passing on of female wisdom and the teachings of the shared community is long gone, but thankfully not lost. The remembering, awakening and reclaiming of the old ways is happening. It is being driven by the very real desire and craving for the connection to each other and the support we need. 21st century living is not connected, we are all separated living in insular units, judging one another and hiding our truths. It's destructive and unhealthy. We are striving rather than thriving, the decline of mental health is testament to this. We live in our heads and online, comparing ourselves unfavourably to others. Especially in the past year with the pandemic shifting life onto *Zoom* for the majority of interactions. Where the internet has become a life line for many, the physical connection is on the wane.

It's no wonder the Maiden years are so conflicting. The messages sent out to all are that girls are princesses to be saved. Firstly she's her Daddy's Princess then growing up to be a "good girl". Any boy or young man who dares show interest in wanting to date a girl has seen the slew of memes around having to face Daddy and his shotgun, the Daddy who wants to lock his little girl up until she's 35. This isn't new. Obviously these are attempts at humour but the subliminal message is that chastity and remaining pure are the most important aspects of respectability. **For a girl!** Good girls don't, sluts / whores / slags / tramps / easy girls do, but if you don't you're frigid. Don't love yourself, you stuck up cow. Flirt and enjoy yourself or be promiscuous and you obviously deserve to be scorned. Ambition is synonymous with hard faced, woman hating bitch sleeping her way to the top. Have children in your teen years ruining your life, but not having kids in teens or twenties is leaving it a bit late, tick tock, old girl. Fat shaming is apparently justified when the epitome of beauty is skinny with jutting collar bones, a thigh gap, big boobs and a pout that looks like a swollen vulva...but don't be skinny because real women have curves. Your entire existence has to be captured, filtered and posted online but if you do then you're only doing it for attention. WTAF!?!

The Maiden years are a bloody minefield with all this toxicity. And it is *everywhere.*

How do you remember your own Maiden teen years or your 20's? Maybe you are in your Maiden years right now.

My Maiden phase was pretty standard for the most part in my teens during the 1990's before becoming more wild and footless in my 20's and the aptly named "naughties" decade. My menarche was a complete non event followed by years of irregular but heavy cycles and awful cramps managed initially by popping *Ponstan* like *Smarties* then the GP putting me on the pill. I had a real desire as a teenager to be arrested, not for anything bad, no, I did NOT want to go to jail, but really thought it would be so cool to be arrested for something I believed in, like *Greenpeace*. I fell into the comparison trap and viewed my work as 'less than' which meant I changed my direction of where I wanted to study after school, ending up picking the wrong course at the wrong university and dropping out. I worked from the age of 14 after securing my first job in the local newsagents. Having my own money and the sense of independence it gave me, ensured I was never out of work. I had good friends, a few boyfriends and my first love in my teens. I also got my first tattoos, Japanese symbols inked on my back. I blame the *Spice Girls* (specifically Mels B and C who inspired my choice). In my twenties, I had a couple of bouts of depression, behaved in a reckless manner with carefree abandon, was super secretive, made friends and lost friends, was confused by what I thought were the "shoulds" versus my wants/needs. I was incredibly insecure but covered it well with my gobby and outgoing personality. I craved independence and individuality, made highly questionable choices, accrued too much debt, and was incapable of living my natural feminine truth instead struggling and failing to be more masculine in my career (I'm not made that way and it made me ill trying, several times). I job hopped many times, sometime working two jobs, but the pattern of the work was that I always got jobs that were well paying but were not the right fit for me, I just saw the £ signs and could nail an interview. I never once went into an interview thinking I wouldn't get it, I just needed to find what it was that I wanted to do. Even when I interviewed for a very well known global airline; I went to London on my 20th birthday, got through the group selection of 20 people, whittled down to me and one other, I was all dolled up in the red uniform and they did my make up ready for the final interview. I was so pleased with myself, I had this in the bag until they told me the training would be starting at the same time I was meant to be on holiday with my mates in Florida. It did not go down well when asked if I would cancel my holiday and I inquired as to at who's expense... needless to say that put the kibosh on that job and I was actually stunned and disappointed I didn't get it. Hmmmph!

Generally my twenties were a messy affair. Don't get me wrong, in amongst the messes, I had many a great time, wild times. I worked hard and played harder with some fantastic memories and a stunning collection of shoes. I tend to regard that time as living a *Sex and the City* lifestyle on a New Look budget! The support network during that period was from different friends at different times, those friends who were also trying to figure out and negotiate their own messes at the same time. What we needed were not role models on camera who were more often than not, neurotic, but guidance from a real, trusted and respected source(s).

The support the Maiden needs is in the form of an established circle of elders, older, experienced mentors, whether that be her mother or another trusted source within the Circle (see Thread 4), one both the Maiden and her mother trust. She also finds the support from the collective Circle. I did have my Mum and we were, still are, close. In my teenage Maiden years, my Mum, the one about who I moaned about was over protective, was the one who looked after my drunk friends (mine and my sister's). She never judged, she just made sure we/they were safe and handed out her hangover "it'll kill you or cure you" remedy in the morning. But as I got older and into my twenties, I was striving to carve out who I thought I was, differentiating myself from who I thought I was expected to be and that did not involve seeking my mum's advice. Thankfully towards the end of my Maiden years I had grown into myself, and was comfortable and secure in the woman I was at that time. This may or may not have been aided by meeting and marrying my husband; he saw me for who I was, and loved me for me, quirks and all, and I didn't need to pretend I was anything other than myself, it was so freeing and liberating.

The Maiden in the spring time is associated with the element of air, the direction of the east with the dawn of the sun and winds of change. Her colours are white and green. She is joyful, dream filled and fresh as she learns to step into her personal power. The power of knowing and understanding her worth, her strengths, her values and her potential. Empowerment embodied.

Now, I ask you to remember the feeling from earlier, about your own experience of your Menarche and life through the Maiden years. Do you still feel the same, or have you changed your mind?

Mother

Mother; such a loaded word. We all have one. We were all birthed from our mother's womb, whether or not we know her. Mother; we will all be one whether or not we have have children.

The Mother archetype is the second phase in a woman's life, following on from the Maiden phase. Typically, the Mother years span our 30's, our caring, protecting, nurturing decade when we are in full bloom. This phase is archetypal of and embodies the mindset, maturity, emotions and feelings of the "Mother". Of course, there will be an overlap between the phases for many women as some will be Mothers at 16 years old or not until 45 years old, and some either through choice or otherwise, never become a "Mum". A child of 12 may end up as living the Mother phase of her life before she even comes into the Maiden phase if the responsibility of caring for a parent or sibling falls on her young shoulders. What does the word Mother mean for you in relation to where you are in your life?

I am a woman, I have birthed a child, therefore in the

eyes of the world I am a "Mother" but it doesn't define me, it is not all of who I am. I am more than, and need more than, the role of Mum. To paraphrase the words of my good friend Holly Elissa; "Some women are to motherhood what Meryl Streep or Dame Judi Dench are to acting". I am not one of those women. Personally I've found the mothering phase of life the most challenging and uncomfortable and it certainly hasn't come easily or naturally (as I naively thought it would). It has also flown past at a ridiculous speed. It is a true saying that the days are long but the years short, when it comes to my Mother phase.

Who is She then, the Mother? Is She an archetype upon a pedestal, such as Demeter or Mother Mary? Is She the Creatrix of all things? Is She the vessel? Is She unknown? Is She a deep wound? Or is She to be categorised and recognised from a whole host of labels including: stay at home mum, working mum, pushy mum, adopted mum, step mum, tiger mum, elephant mum, helicopter mum, over protective mum, negligent mum, judgmental mum, good mum, holier-than-thou mum, anxious mum, yummy mum(my), slobby mum, narcissistic mum, loving mum, competitive mum, barely holding it together mum, PTA mum, disappointed mum, first-time mum, doing-the-best-she-can-mum, earth mum(ma), hippie mum, IVF mum, exhausted mum, natural mum, teen mum, old mum, geriatric (in the UK, pregnant women over the age of 36 are referred to as geriatric...charming) mum, child-less woman, lesbian mum, single mum, busy mum, selfish mum, frazzled mum, surrogate mum, absent mum... I'm sure there are 100 more labels that I have missed that could be added. (My son says I am an embarrassing mum, but he's obviously wrong). But is that really who She is? To be honest I could be any one of the majority of that list depending upon when my parenting was under review and by whom!

The Mother phase may not seem applicable to some as

they have chosen not to, or are unable to have children, but that does not rule out the Mother in all of us. She is the Creatrix of life; be that of children, career, project, and of yourself! However you choose and what ever you create in this life, you are the Mother of that creation.

This phase of our lives is possibly the most judged; we're damned if we do and damned if we don't! Your choices here are up for discussion and scrutiny whether you like it and know it or not. But why is this the case? Society and of course, Patriarchy.

The role of Mother is valued and equally not valued. Our fertile years carry an expectation that we will reproduce whilst at the same time we are judged for staying at home to raise our own children or comment is passed that we have returned to the workplace instead of being at home. To stay at home is a luxury and is seen as not be participating in or contributing to economic growth of the society, yet to work is seen as a fault as we expect the state, grandparents or strangers to raise our kids whilst we are at work. It's a no-win situation. And that is without the gender pay gap that maternity leave wrongfully exacerbates via unscrupulous and manipulative employers. You will of course be no stranger to the fact that this is specific purely to mothers; fathers are not subjected to such restrictions, judgments or expectations. Do you remember when Holly Willoughby stood in for Ant McPartlin on *I'm a Celebrity, Get Me Out of Here* in 2018? The papers were aghast. What will happen to Holly's kids whilst she's away in Australia filming for 3 weeks? Yet at the same time, Holly's co-presenter, Declan Donnelly, had just become a brand new first time daddy but not a whisper appeared in print about what would happen to his new born whilst he was away for 3 weeks! Fathers are not expected to factor in family considerations when it comes to career, just the mothers.

Should you be child-free/childless during these 'fertile'

years, you are not free from probing questions and judgement either - regardless of how inappropriate or hurtful the interrogation. Should you only have one child, face being questioned about when you're having more and that "an only child is a lonely child" but have four or more kids and then the questions become about your sex life and potential lack of a telly in the house. "My body, my choice, my business - fuck off and mind your own" is not, however, regarded as a suitable answer by these judgey types. The flow of the caustic opine is purely one way.

Whilst the Mother is pregnant, in current society, she is revered, fawned over and strangers have a desire to touch your ever growing belly, sans permission. A pregnant woman is celebrated. That is until the baby is born, then the focus shifts. This is the time when Mothers are at their most vital, most important, most in need and most vulnerable, yet this is the time when your role begins its demise in patriarchal society. Your appearance and actions are now being judged. Mother is on the pedestal and every expectation not met is a failing to be scorned. Having just binged watched the first eight series of *Call The Midwife* again on *Netflix*, I feel incredibly nostalgic for the care, respect and encouragement the women received from the Nonnatus Nuns and the midwives (not so much for the conditions the people were living in and some of the legislation of the time however). The mothers were the focus and were cared for as well as their babes whilst being viewed as strong, capable and vital!

I am no stranger to judgement; being judged and judging others. It's not pretty from either side but it's there and it runs deep. We judge others from our own insecurities and we hurt beyond belief when on the receiving end which further fuels the judgement cycle. Or maybe that's just me. As a new mum I was excruciatingly anxious and defensive (which took me by surprise) and as a result, super judgemental of how others were doing it which in turn inflamed my own insecurities. I am thoroughly embarrassed by it now and ashamed. It cost me friendship and fed into what I now realise to have most probably have been undiagnosed post natal depression then sliding into low level depression and anxiety, living constantly on the defensive and my nerves. But like many mothers, we become martyrs, swallow it down keep going, and tell no-one. Smile!

The first couple of years embodying the Mother archetype, I found, were wonderful. I felt powerful, assertive, I knew my own mind. When I fell pregnant I was on cloud nine. I freaking LOVED being pregnant, every bit of it. I think I was glowing for those 9 months like the kid off of the *Ready Brek* adverts. A woman I worked with commented that she had never known anyone to love rubbing their bump as much me – I couldn't keep my hands off it! But the first four years of my mothering journey with my child were the loneliest and lowest points of my life, not helped by miscarrying our second baby; a grief that took eight years to get over, until I was 40 and knew that we were 100% not having any more children. It took eight years to reach that acceptance. I know for others, however, the acceptance never comes.

In my experience, the latter years of the Mother archetype are more akin to the initial ones and that came from experience and finding an inner strength and grit that I never knew I possessed. It's the increased self confidence to believe in yourself, to establish your boundaries, prioritise what's important, accept you're not perfect and neither is life and let the situations, opinions and people that don't align, just jog on. Finding happiness, contentment and joy within yourself and within your own familial, friendship or relationship bubble makes navigating Mother phase challenges so much easier. As does picking the right battles not all the battles.

Grieve the loss of your Maiden years.

Reaching the Mother phase and beyond of our life cycle means letting go of the previous phase; the Maiden years. Do you ever look back at the young woman you once were? Think about the decisions you made (or didn't make), miss the youth you once had, cringe at actions or words, feel pain for situations, long for the freedom enjoyed, the body you had or the life you lived? Maybe you are still in your maiden years? Or maybe they are but a distant memory?

As we grow and evolve and learn and experience, we change. We become who we are, and who we are may well be a completely different person to who we were. It is perfectly OK to grieve for the woman we once were. She is you, part of you that will forever live on in you and your memory, she is just no longer part of your present. And that's as it is. Grieve for her, love her and set her free while loving the you you are now. Moving from the Maiden to the Mother is not necessarily an easy transition. We are older, with different priorities to our Maiden years, many of us have way more responsibilities too. Raising children, caring for elderly parents or other relatives, supporting friends and sisters with their children, birthing and working in careers, starting and building our own businesses, running our homes and countless other responsibilities that tend to fall on us at this time. With that extra load, it is absolutely necessary to grieve the loss of our Maiden years and its freedoms if you feel called to. We wear our tiredness as a badge of honour and medicate with wine or gin. Societal conditioning plays its part here too with the expectation of us to be selfless in the quest to achieve and do it all. There is also the expectation of the yummy mummy aesthetic to contend with, which is kept sustained by the media. It is a damn site harder to maintain the Maiden physique in the Mother years. Our bodies don't just snap back into their Maiden mould post-partum, because they aren't supposed to!

There is so much wisdom, joy, celebration and beauty in these years to cherish. (Despite my moans). If I could do this section of my life over again, I absolutely would, but with the head I have on my shoulders now.

How can we ensure that the Mother years are the positive experience they ought to be? How to cultivate that supportive and nurturing environment? You just know what I'm going to say...*Circle*!

THIS is one of those times in life when your circle, community, support network of sisters, is your life line. Whether a circle of women you gather with regularly in sacred space, or a specific Mother's Circle, the Red Tent support is there waiting to hold you when you need it. There is no advice unless its asked for but there is plenty of time to be heard and held. You can be honest and let out the shadow side without judgement and are encouraged to share ALL aspects of this Mother energy - the good, the bad, the struggles and the victories. The fellow women in Circle will have been there or going through it similarly. You also have the opportunity to pay this back when the time comes for other women who need the support. It is connection to peers interwoven between generations and differing experiences. There are are many things we would love to say or admit but can't because the fear of judgment. And judgement surrounding mothering or the choice not to become a "Mother" is one of the worst and most deeply felt. Had I had the circle in place back when I entered the Mother phase, my own journey would have been dramatically different. I know that to be a fact.

As I mentioned, my experience in the early years of this phase was my loneliest in my life. I went from being confident and self assured at 31, to birthing my son and experiencing a 180 degree flip in my personality. When I needed support the most, when at the most vulnerable and lost, self conscious and lacking in self confidence and ability to be the Mother I wanted to be, I was without the support I needed. Despite knowing lots of people, I didn't have close friends, and I didn't initially have the confidence to make any new ones either, for a good few of years. I hated the Mother & Baby/Toddler groups as they exhausted me, using all my energy to be happy and chatty and trying to include myself but they felt cliquey and a yummy mummy I ain't! I had my Mum (without whom I would never have gotten through those initial years as I did) and mother in law, both of whom were supportive in their own way, but these two women did not a Circle make. Once I started believing and trusting in myself again and my capabilities, forcing myself out to meet new people - and finding the right ones - my life changed. The group of women who became my Circle were treasured and invaluable, not just to me but to one another - our support was collective and given amongst each other as needed.

Just think what the Maiden and Mother years would look like if circles where caring, sharing and supporting each other were the norm rather than the judgement and criticism faced in isolation.

The Mother phase is the full moon stage of the lunar cycle; full belly, luminous, beautiful and glorious. She is fully in protection mode, healing and receiving. She is radiant with health and well being, she is captivating. You are captivating. She is a wonder. You are a wonder. Magic. The Mother phase is ovulation, our inner summer. This is our most fertile time, when we have the most energy and are feeling super charged, super sexy, confident and magnetic. (Ironically, I'd wager more mum's feel super knackered, frumpy, insecure, full of doubt and second guessing themselves during the "mother" phase!) Her symbolic colour is red.

We are living with the lessons we learned during our Maiden's journey. We are wiser, older, more aware of who we are and what our values and priorities are.

Wild Woman

Who is Wild Woman? Is she Lilith? Jezebel? Mary Magdalene? Asherah? Salome? Medusa? Rhiannon? Mogain Le Fey? Cerridwen? The Morrighan? Artemis? Diana? Samantha off of *Sex and the City*? Is She the one who runs with the wolves? Is She ...You? Welcome the Wild Woman. The Enchantress, the Queen, the Witch, Bitch, Matriarch or Mage. It doesn't matter what you call her. She is real and this phase of our lives needs acknowledging. We hold our power once we reclaim it and honour it for ourselves and each other.

The Wild Woman age roughly spans years 42-63 with, of course, plenty room for overlap from the previous Mother phase. It's our time to take and make space for ourselves, turn inwards to nurture ourselves and get to know ourselves better (going to drop self care in here). Many women find that this is also when they become more interested in a personal spiritual practice or are curious to find out what life means to them. This might include understanding and learning to trust their own intuition or tracing family lineage for example. I found that pull to know where I came from incredibly powerful. The answers I uncovered were both surprising and yet made so much sense to who I am, leading me to understand the blood that runs in my veins.

We can reclaim who we are.

When I turned forty, I considered it to be the next chapter in this life. 40, yes, it is just another number, an arbitrary age, but to me it was more than that. It felt like a completely new start; the dawn of the next phase in this life cycle, a rite of passage, with new lessons to learn and experiences to have and I jolly well welcomed it. The Wild Woman phase. I am currently straddling the phases of Mother and the Wild Woman. The Mother phase has ended from the point of view that I am done with the actual birthing of little humans but is still very much part of my every day existence as I focus on the raising my tweenager. It is definitely not over completely as I have many projects yet to birth, including this book that I am writing and the other ones that are waiting to be written. The Wild Woman part of me knows who she is. I trust myself and am accepting of who I am and of what I have achieved and done (not all with pride or without regret, but with acceptance nonetheless). There remain parts of me that continue to be a work in progress; things I want to achieve and accomplish or release and that will likely continue as I cross off more that I do to be replaced by new challenges and goals, dreams and desires. I have never before felt so confident in and comfortable with who I am as I do right now. Middle age is ace!

We are never too old or too late to do what or be who we want.

Our forties represent the journey into the autumn years of life, that magical time when we are in transition between the Mother and the Crone; the perimenopausal years moving from our fertile mothering years into that where we connect truly with who we are as women, owning our own person. Of course not every woman takes until she's 40 to reach this place of knowing herself, but I did, and have been on this journey of self discovery for a long time.

Personally, I love this phase, it's my favourite! It is also my favourite part of my inner cycle and in the annual cycle outside in nature. Life is such a celebration and our autumn years are no exception. When I was in my Maiden phase, my "scary age" was 35, but since my late 30's I couldn't wait for my 40's. I turned forty, three years ago, and I have to say it has been worth the wait! It is a true saying that *Life Begins At 40*. There was for me, a distinct shift inside that went from self consciously hiding my truth, people pleasing and a need to be liked, to being thoroughly honest with myself, unapologetic in being exactly who I am and stopping pussyfooting around others so as not offend them or make them uncomfortable, at my expense. And yes, it has been both noticed and not always liked. But too bad! My transition phase started with the shedding and letting go of outside judgement and the placing of my value and worth in those external hands. I don't mean that being true and honest gives us carte blanche to be a total twat, our field of fucks is not so barren, I just mean choose what you care about wisely and release the rest that does not serve or only brings you unnecessary drama.

This phase covers our blood-rite; the transitioning perimenopause years leading into menopause. Or to give it its other name, "Moon Pause". It's an intense time where you feel all the feels in all their glory! Rage, hot flushes, insomnia, depression, lower sex drive, or swing to the other extreme of super charged sex drive, headaches, increasingly irregular periods and mood swings are some of the most common "symptoms" of a transition in our lives that has been medicalised and medicated. We are not allowed to feel and experience this natural change in our bodies without being dismissed, misdiagnosed or told we need antidepressants. According to the NHS website, the majority of women move through this stage around age 48-52 but some begin much earlier (like me) or start later - there is no right or wrong time, just as there is no predetermined timescale for the perimenopause. I am embracing my perimenopause; deepening the journey into knowing myself. Acknowledging my needs and accepting the changes is a gift I give to myself with honour and love.

However, it is also during this time sadly, when we are most likely to be called hormonal, hysterical, possibly even bi-polar(!) and most definitely a bitch. Lovely.

Why? Because women are meant to be and equally not meant to be, everything except for who we are!! Because middle aged women are viewed as less than the Mother (but more than the Crone) and vastly diminished and practically worthless compared to the Maiden. Incase you missed the memo, we are no longer "worth it". Over 40 or worse, over 50, no, no, no, that won't do. The Maiden is idolised for her youth but not her experience. We are plied with adverts everywhere about eternal youth, staying young looking, even to "age well" by using anti-ageing lotions and potions! What's so wrong with saying: "Hey, I'm 40 (or 50, or 60 +) and I'm ageing. I know I'm ageing well because I am alive and living and have the life experience to prove it!!" Instead you're supposed to keep your mouth shut, don't create a scene, don't age, stay young and look young but don't look like you're trying to look young! Oh Pu-lease!!

Many of us were wild and free in our Maiden years, wild with abandon and lack of responsibility. The wild of the Wild Woman years is wild from self empowerment, self knowing, from casting off the shackles of expectation and conditioning. The Wild Woman comes in to her own when she respects herself and doesn't placate others to the detriment of herself. There comes a time when you realise that no, you aren't in a bad mood but in fact refusing to accept the bullshit and judgement just to please others and make them feel comfortable. When people pleasing has always been the (my) default, some struggle to accept the change when that is no longer the case.

Now we are taking back our power as our sovereign right. It's a metamorphosis; a thing of beauty, but, in reclaiming this wild it may mean leaving behind those who will not support or "approve" of your growth. And wild is being okay with that. Acceptance. The wildness is yours to reclaim, embrace and own. Step into yourself, there is your power.

Autumn is so glorious from all its facets, can we please embrace and give reverence to women in their own autumn too? This is truly a spectacular age that is not to be feared or disregarded, but celebrated for the wise, wild, unabashed, unashamed, knowledgeable and powerful women that we are.

Can you imagine how incredible it would be if you were part of a Women's Sacred Circle which honoured the phases of our life cycle and allowed each of us to be held, heard and honoured in our respective phases? How different might the world be if Wild Autumn Women took their place, sat in their power, and got on with living, without the prescribed shoulds and expectations?

Circles are invaluable in my experience. They are as abundant in support and love as autumn fruits and give you the necessary hygge coziness you need to sustain you through the deepening darkness into winter. A space where your Wild Woman is not only welcomed but appreciated too, where your sisters hold space for your Wild Woman to emerge as unshakeable, integral and sacred, where you can then ground into the deepest knowing of your unique feminine soul.

I feel enormously lucky to be living in this time as my generation are reclaiming their perimenopause years by sharing their stories, experiences, the good, the bad, the sweaty and the sublime. No more hiding and being embarrassed or confused or misdiagnosed. Our transformation is ours, is magnificence embodied, and with the potential to terrify a large swathe of the population... hmm, suddenly everything become clear!

Wild Woman, rise!
Wild Women, together, we rise!

With a deep regal purple the Wild Woman is recognised. Autumn is her season; the premenstrual phase of your cycle, the perimenopause phase in your life. Your most powerful aspect is out to play and she is both warrior and protector of her sovereignty, try her if you dare, but beware, you'll get honesty, integrity, a solid dose of realism with little to no patience or tolerance for fools and nonsense. We meet our shadow here where it forces us to see what we would rather not and makes us choose; either hide from it or face it and deal with it. The season of the witch honours the waning phase of the moon, the acceptance of the second half of life, the journey towards the end (which is inevitable in all forms of life). The energy is introspective and contemplative, assessing what has gone before and what is yet to come, meeting and facing the shadows. Where the spring and summer, Maiden and Mother energies are light, bright and optimistic, the autumn and winter, Wild Woman and Crone are dark, deep and questioning.

Now in my forties and I have taken stock and reassessed where and who I am. It's like a fresh page, the restart of knowing and understanding who I am but with the actual experience behind me. While I no longer harbour ambitions to become an interior designer (my teenage career choice) I am still creative and need to express that. I know what I want to do, am just finding the confidence to push past the imposter complex to achieve my dreams, starting with writing this book. Instead of being sad and melancholy over *what ifs* or *shoulds*, I am grateful for the experiences I have had and the lessons learned as I am sat here, a woman who has lived, loved, lost and laughed. A lot! We are who we are because of ourselves. We can't change our past, but we can learn from it and grow from there. This second half of life will be all the richer for it.

Crone

The Grandmother, the Elder Woman, the Sage, the Wise Woman with her crown of grey and white hair, the Crone. Who is she? She is a life time of memories, of life's ups and downs. She has weathered storms a plenty and got the wrinkles and scars to prove it! She is the sum total of all she has experienced and is shaped by those experiences. She is a lived, aged, seasoned woman of worth.

Crone is synonymous with hag, auld wummin, old woman, auld croney and ugly, evil witch. Basically negative and unwanted associations. Urgh, are we done with that trope yet? We are so over it! Who wants yo thought of as a Crone? Well, I do when my time comes but not in the *Disney* version, thanks very much. Instead can we flip the whole stereotype and reframe it in a positive light? I love Gloria Steinem's thought on the matter:

"Women become more radical with age. One day an army of grey haired women may quietly take over earth."

The imagery that quote creates in my head is one of Violet Crawley, the Dowager Countess of Grantham (*Downton Abbey*) and Sophia Petrillo (*The Golden Girls*) leading their troops to a mass gathering of the Women's Council, where they put the world to right with their unfiltered straight talking and a wit as caustic as the soda used by their maid or mother to unblock kitchen drains. Ooft! Powerful.

The phase of the Crone comes into herself post menopausally, but the old women of yesteryear are not who I see as the older women today. So other than the menopause, what defines a Crone in the 21st century? Just as the previous archetypes and phases may be experienced outwith the Maiden to Mother to Matriarch pattern, so too may the Crone. I have a friend who is younger than me but exudes sage Crone energy and is wise far beyond her chronological years.

This is an enormously juicy and deep topic waiting to be discussed and liberated. What do you think? When it comes to considering the senior years in life I have far more questions than I do answers. I want to hear about the experience and views of the elder women in today's society, to hear what they think about modern life, how they feel they are viewed by society, the challenges they face, how their lives are different from or the same as the crones that they had in their lives when they were younger women and how their lives were different from or the same as the younger women today. Their voices are vital and need to be heard. Not shooshed and dismissed.

The wise, elder women in our families and towns and cities cannot continue to be (not that they ever should have been) identified as irrelevant, insignificant, obsolete, daft, old-fashioned or simply put, just old! Older women tend to be regarded in one of two ways, either as a nice wee biddy or as a grumpy old battleaxe and tend not respected or revered for their wisdoms and experiences, often considered to be ignorant of today's issues facing the younger generation, therefore don't know anything. Seriously? How does that make you feel to look at those adjective describing your future or your life currently? This is not how I view the elder women in my life.

Let us explore the Wise Woman / Crone / Elder / Grandmother years. Not from the societal view of an invisible meek wee old lady, but the powerful, valuable women they are!

Power to the Crone!

As I said I have more questions than I do answers, so I took my questions to crones I know and asked them:

What is the best thing about being an older woman today?

"More often than not it's the women who are left widowed, and we are in a comfortable position providing the husband took care of the finances earlier on. When we have our health we can relax in a reasonably well off situation."

"Not having the same issue the young ones face today with the pressures of social media, mental health problems, peer pressure etc. It's a scary time. I worry for the young people today. We had peer pressure in my day but it was completely different and the whole world didn't know about it. I would not want to be young today."

"I don't have to work and I have my pension. I have all the time in the world to do what I want when I want and enjoy life"

"If you are no longer in the work force, you have much more time for leisure activities"

"The best thing in this 'now' moment is being true to myself. Standing in my truth and having the freedom to do so."

What challenges do you face as an older woman today?

"Technology. Life is too fast these days and no point trying to keep up, especially with the devices, I don't want to use them. The basics of life and how to live are gone."

"The pace, mainly. In my work, it's changing and is a younger person's game now. But my job has been my saviour during the pandemic, why should I have to retire? If women are able, it's not our responsibility to retire when we don't feel ready to."

"My memory isn't as good and I get a bit forgetful."

"Losing mobility and physically no longer to cope without help."

"No less or more challenging of any woman of any age."

What are your thoughts on ageing?

"As I'm getting older I don't feel I'm ageing, just feel perhaps my pace is slower. I don't feel older, compared to my mother's generation who looked older due to effects of the war years. I don't feel there is an expectation to look young from society, but I have personal expectation and standard. I like to look my best when I go out and I enjoy taking care of skin, hair and nails, it makes me feel good if I look good."

"It's never bothered me, I'm happy with myself personally. If you're happy and content with yourself then what does it matter? My only issue with ageing is the criticism from younger generation, especially after raising them!"

"It's rubbish, I want to stay as young as ever I was. Although I do think older women are more accepting of the ageing process as it happens"

"Staying active is important, mentally and physically. Getting out for a daily walk and gardening as well as joining social groups (e.g. book group or art class) and reading books I didn't have time for when bringing up my family."

What advice do you have for younger women today?

"Go out and have a life and exceed your own expectations to the best of your ability, and if they don't work then at least you tried. Go and have the best life you can, things will come up you don't expect and you deal with them the best you can. The opportunities are there, be flexible in your choices and enjoy life."

"Be themselves and try take life day by day and not dig up any worries unnecessarily. Be flexible and not take comments or criticism personally."

"Young folk are a bit backwards in coming forward when it comes to asking for help. I would say to stop looking for things or problems that aren't there. Take each day as it comes, one day at a time and deal with the challenges you face. There is always a solution. Stop focussing on the negatives and look on the bright side on life."

"Before deciding upon a career path think carefully about what you have a passion for and pursue that as a job which you will enjoy. Believe that you are capable of succeeding in any challenge that you set yourself."

How are elder women viewed by society today compared to in your mother's day?

"Just the same. There is a generation gap which has stayed. Maybe now we are expected to move with the times, but in my Mother's day they weren't."

"They were seen as old. Just that; old. But today we aren't simply "old", we are older and that is a positive thing. I don't feel old and I still have plenty life in me yet."

"I feel the 70+ are overlooked and often forgotten."

"Women were older years ago, they had an older outlook, old fashioned frame of mind, and no interests outside of the house. Young people respected the elders, not that they don't respect us now, but instead we are treated more like a friend. I like that."

"I think older women are well regarded for what they have to offer in life experience."

Who were your role models as a young woman?

"The hard working farmer's wife; very domesticated, she focussed on her home and children. Also my own Mother, who was not material minded, [materialistic] but content and happy with her lot."

"My mother used to babysit for the lady across the road, who was a single mum. I saw her all ready to go out one time, and her hair was all done and she had a big brimmed hat, a dress with the stiff petticoat to make it stick out, black patent stilettos that looked like rainbows of colour shining on them and her handbag over her shoulder. She *looked like a movie star. I used to like Doris Day too and the dresses she wore, so feminine compared to today's dresses."*

How has the life of an older woman improved in the modern day compared with your mother's generation?

"Mod cons. Life is far easier compared to my Mother's generation with modern technology in the homes. My Mother had a hard life, no time for family life and children and hobbies. It was all physical chores."

"I have a voice. I'm self sufficient, financially."

"Mod cons. Do women today appreciate them?"

"Care for the elderly, specifically home appliances which make life easier, at home care, volunteer groups to help with transport etc and food delivery services."

"More money, our own money not our man's money. We are far better off. Gone are the days living off the housekeeping handed out by the husband and a wee holiday with that week's wages, not able save."

How has the view of and experience of the menopause changed in society?

"People are more aware now, it's better, and will help the younger ones today compared to the old way. You are able to talk to people, and be open about it now, not hidden. In my day we were told to just go for a walk"

"It's not hidden now. It was terrible when my mother was

young, nobody talked about it, all. Even periods weren't discussed, I thought something was wrong with me the first time I took mine. My Mam from then on used to ask me each month if I was "no well" yet".

"It's a huge step forward that 'menstruation' is no longer a 'taboo' subject and gets covered by the media about how disabling it can be for some women and embarrassing for women in a business career."

So, what do you think? Were the responses what you expected? I enjoyed having these conversations and getting an insight from the points of view of the crones in my life.

My Mum is in her mid sixties but neither looks, acts or more importantly, *feels* old. She is a feisty woman who doesn't suffer fools; she is strong, opinionated and judgemental (where do you think I learned it?), glamorous incredibly loving and fiercely maternal. She is a lioness when it comes to her family; turns out so was her own mother! She is my role model despite her abject horror that I'm excited about my grey hairs and desire to grow them not dye them. My 80 year old Mother in Law (who could easily pass for a decade younger and has amazing skin) is different to my Mum though just as vocal in her opinions and judgements. She has a quiet strength and possesses an unflappable steadiness that doesn't get excited or fazed about, or by, anything. She has taught me valuable lessons about being content, living the small simple life without rush, without fuss, where everything that needs to be done gets done when you slow down and take your time. One thing I definitely took away from the questions is confirmation that "old" today is not the same as "old" in generations gone by. Going forward I don't see this or future generations going quietly into the grey mists of time.

When I first moved to the village I currently live in, I popped into the local library where there was a women's group deep in discussion. They clearly met regularly to chat. I overheard parts of their discussion as I was browsing the shelves: one was needing new fishnet tights, one needed tartan bows to stitch onto her knickers, one had signed up for a fire eating course (I wanted to ask where she'd signed up) followed by a grinding course! Another was talking about her dancing, all this was mixed with what they were having for their tea later. The average age of this group of around seven ladies was about 70! Brilliant! Never underestimate the Crones!

The Crone is represented by the Dark Moon phase, the colour black, the season of winter, by our menstrual blood and by the post menopausal years. Her energy is slow, reflective, resting, internal and wise. She is the guardian between the worlds, between life and death. She is not to be feared but revered.

As we celebrate post menopausal women and the women we will become, have a think about who the wise women in your life are. What influence have they had on the elder woman you will become? I encourage you to delve into the soul of your being, seek the truth and reclaim the Crone, become the wise woman and let us rise up sovereign, together!

You are the Maiden, Mother, Matriarch and Crone, continually cycling and spiralling. Each phase an expression of a life being lived.

One topic that is never far away when discussing women, particularly women over the age of 30 (!) is the topic of ageing. How do you view ageing? What hang-ups, if any, do you have about ageing? What does being an older woman mean to you?

I took to Instagram and my newsletter for research purposes and asked how women today view ageing and menopause. I was delighted the the overall age positivity:

What are your thoughts on ageing?

"A beautiful and powerful process to step into you."

"If you are no longer in the work force, you have much more time for leisure activities."

"I have never fussed about the number or the way my body is changing. However now I'm 35, there's something niggling away at me about all the things like children and becoming a home owner etc. I worry I'm running out of time."

"Embrace it, the media makes us feel like it's unnatural and not a symbol of how we've grown."

"We are fed by society that it's not great and are set up to reverse the ageing process. There's money in that."

"I think I'm getting younger, lol."

"Happy to be ageing. I feel wiser and more sure of myself. I hate the slurs like 'Karen', of being seen as busybodies with nothing to do/say of value."

"I see ageing as a natural process and I have always since a young girl been desperate to be old."

"I think the ageing process can be liberating, I feel less pressure to be a certain way, dress, size, hair cut etc, I feel people see you as less threat so you can get away with more."

"Society's view of old means weak, with not much to contribute, but truthfully the feminine skills are vastly under valued."

How do you regard the menopause?

"Empowering AF!"

"I don't think about it to be honest."

"It should be taught to kids alongside puberty. It's always been described in most horrendous ways, having women think they are crackpots. Needs to be looked at properly and shown how empowering it can be."

"I long for the menopause in so many ways but have yet to understand the actual process as my gran died when I was very little and my mom had a hysterectomy. So I need more knowledge of it."

"Angrily. Not by the menopause but how I was treated by (female) GP when I went for help. I was fobbed off, but when I went back again couple of years later the experience was completely different because now, that same GP was going through the menopause herself!"

Interestingly, as I sat editing this section, there was a discussion happening on *Loose Women* on the telly in the background regarding grey hair and going grey. According to some survey Kaye Adams was quoting, women with grey hair are considered to be warm, but incompetent!! The invisibility of women is enhanced by the greying of the hair. WTF???

I am LOVING the ageing process. I am firmly anti anti-ageing. My grey hairs are joyous (not just because they are wavy and I have always wanted wavy/curly hair having lived 40+ years with poker straight locks, never needing hair straighteners in my life, woe betide any hairdresser that came near me with them. Even when I got my hair permed at 12 years old for starting high school, it was straight again two days later!!!), my wrinkles are well earned, particularly those laughter lines, my life's experiences grant me wisdom and I do not wish to be 20 again! I feel lucky to have had an analogue childhood/adolescence and digital adulthood. It is the perfect combination for this life, I don't think I could do or would even want to do my teens or twenties online *shudders*. What happened in the nineties and naughties stays in the nineties and naughties! I am "acting my age" (what ever that means), 43, as I live and breathe it - I don't know how else to do it! The older I get, the more I like, love and respect myself and everything that I am, which is an honour sadly not lived by all. It's not bad or wrong or an entitlement to age (dis)gracefully – it is a bloody privilege!

A self that goes on changing is a life that goes on living
~ Virginia Woolf ~

The more we experience and learn, the more we grow and evolve. This is a good thing. Our bodies evolve and transform as we grow up, through puberty, pregnancy (if applicable), through to the menopause (2nd puberty) and beyond. Each phase and stage comes with its frustrations, anxieties, insecurities, negative connotations and misinformation or taboos. Understanding the processes helps us to see the beauty unfolding. Change can be courageous. Change can be acceptance. Change can be self belief. Change can be challenging old thought patterns and stigmas. Change is life.

All life is a cycle of phases, moving from one to next to the next, sometimes in a logical pattern, of Maiden to Mother to Matriarch to Crone as the seasons follow one another but also sometimes from Mother to Maiden to Matriarch to Mother to Maiden to Crone, depending on what is happening in life at that point, depending where life is taking us and what we are required to do. Every ending is simply a new beginning with the additional benefit of experience, wisdom and confidence. It's the perpetual spiral, in and out, evolving with each cycle. Nothing is certain, definite or predetermined, other than the fact that one day we will all draw our last breath. What we do in the time prior to that moment, how we experience the time we have is, for the most part, up to us.

Death; Life's Only Certainty.

Death. The final phase of this life. The Close. Why do we fear it? Why do we shield our children from it, disconnect and disassociate from it, not talk about it until it's too late, treat it as taboo?

This wasn't always the way. Just like birth, our dying were cared for and prepared, before and after the death, in the home. (I'm going to guess this would have been a role for the women but am happy to be corrected as I don't know that for sure.) Death is certainly something I've given a lot of thought to over the past few years with losing several family members and friends. How do I personally view and process the end of life, how am I explaining it to my child, am I telling him too much or not enough, am I shielding him and if so why? Lots to ponder when it comes to life's only certainty!

One thing I have realised is that kids really do seem to "get it". Whenever I have told my son about the passing of someone he knew, he has been sad but also bounced back quickly. His first experience of grief was the loss of his Papa, my Father in Law, when he was six. He was upset but blind sided me with his philosophical reaction after the initial tears. In almost the same breath, he wiped his snotty nose sat up straight and asked "so how are babies made?" (how are they *made* not where do they come from!) Cue stuttering mother asking if now was really the time for that conversation? Apparently it was an important question because we all die and we are all born. (Where was this coming from in my then 6 year old's head?) Of course I offered up the one thing I vowed I would never say: "It involves a special cuddle between the mummy and daddy, now time for you to try to get some sleep. We can discuss it later." Jesus wept, Lissa!! In my defence it was one o'clock in the morning. When our very dear friend died from cancer, my son was eight years old, and again was very upset, but he knew it was coming this time. After he settled down from the news he was dreading, he matter of factly stated that "we all die, just at different times, just like animals." When do we lose that sense of perspective and connection to nature and the cycle of life? I had grossly underestimated his capacity for understanding death and dealing with grief, based purely on how I had known and felt about it.

Death has become so sanitised and clinical thanks to the Victorians and I don't think it is healthy or to our benefit. It removes the connection of life and the living from the deceased, it instils fear and morbidity instead of loving reverence. As a result I really think the way death and end of life is viewed and dealt with, causes more problems and makes the grieving process all the more painful. Does that make sense?

Traditionally in Celtic customs, commonly Scottish and Irish, the dead bodies were keened over by the women. Keening is a form of wailing and toning, an outpouring of grief in the form of a choral lament. Women were specifically hired for this role. It was such a powerful practice and is connected to the myths and legends of the Bean sidhe (banshee). Could we bring that back today and incorporate it into today's funeral customs?

Talking about dying and death in every day conversation would potentially make the eventual process far easier to accept and less traumatic to handle, especially if we were able to share what we wanted to happen at our funerals or plans and preparations in the lead up to our deaths. We make birth plans, why not death plans? My own fears and sticking my head in sand when my friend was dying denied her the chance to share fully her own fears and concerns. She wanted to talk about what was going to happen after she was gone, but there I was, full of toxic positive chat of "don't worry", "it'll be fine", "you can do this, the Doctors can do that", that didn't help either of us. I didn't even say good bye on my last visit to the hospice as was clinging on to the hope that I might get another visit despite knowing full well that I wasn't. I deeply regret that now, and instead wish I had just sat, said nothing and listened to her, to her fears, to her plans, to her hopes for the future that she was envisioning for her children, the future that she would never see. We need to release death from the cloak of fear and bring it into the light of day to see it for who it is and what it represents.

Death; as much a part of life as birth.

Time is finite and life is lost. Grief doesn't so much heal the loss felt, as it does shift into a new way of living and continuing on. That ever revolving cycle of life.

Gone
Remember
Individual
Evolution
Forgiveness

Awaken Your Wild You

9

Remember Reconnect Reclaim

Meditation

Spiral into the Cycle

Close your eyes and take a deep breath in through your nose and slowly exhale, releasing through your mouth. On your next inhale, imagine breathing right into your heart space, filling it up with the light of your existence and being. As you exhale, that light radiates out of your heart centre, enveloping your entire body in its glow.

Let's take another breath here, inhale, filling your heart space and exhale radiating your light. Now take your breath and inhale right down into your womb space, your inner cauldron. As you exhale, you ignite your inner flame. Breathe in and fuel those embers. Exhale and feel that fire emanate its power through your body. Take another deep breath in. You are a source of light and power – feel it. And exhale slowly.

Imagine you are outside. Take a moment to observe where you are. What do you see? What time of day is it? What season or weather do you notice? Do you hear anything – maybe birds or traffic or flowing water. Be aware of how you are feeling. (pause for a breath or two)

There is a pathway just a few steps to your side. Walk over to the path. It's an old worn path, a little overgrown at the edges, with grasses and plants. From here it is not clear where this path leads to but you decide you are going to walk it. Standing at the threshold to this path you take a deep calming breath as you consider what possibilities lie ahead. (pause for 1 deep breath)

When you are ready, begin to walk. Take in the scenery – does it change? As you walk this path you notice that you are being led in a spiral but as yet there is no end in sight. Notice too, the speed to which you are walking and why. Notice what thoughts pop into your mind as you step one foot in front of the other in constant rhythm. Notice how your body is feeling; is it light or sluggish, are you holding any pain or tension? (pause for 2 breaths)

Keep walking. Surrender to the journey. (pause for a breath) Notice now how the journey is beginning to change, the time of day has shifted and so too the season from when you started out. How do you feel? What do you see, hear and smell? (pause for a breath) Continue onwards.

You reach the centre of the spiral. Take another deep breath in through your nose and out through your mouth. (pause for 1 deep breath)

You feel a stirring underfoot and now the deepest desires and dreams that reside within begin to stir deep within you too. A fire bursts into life in the very centre of the spiral, recognising and feeding the sister flames of inspiration and passion that are alight around your inner cauldron, whose contents are bubbling in anticipation. (pause for a breath or two)

That stirring you feel both from the earth and yourself is increasing in its power. You feel the need, the want, to shake off all that is holding you back. Shake it off now. Shake it out through your arms and fingers, shake it out down your legs and out the tips of your toes. Allow the shake to take over your body. Shake, woman. Shake! As the shake gains momentum, surrender to it. And release it! SIGH ahhhhhhhhhhhhhhhhhhhhhhhhhhh, exhale.

You are being tested – are you ready to face this challenge, to let it all go? Are you ready to fully grow into yourself, to allow yourself to BE that person? Your plans, goals, desires, dreams are waiting for you. Everything is aligned, just ready for you.

With another deep breath, you take in the glorious sight of the flames as they draw you nearer. What colour are they? What scents do you smell? You know you are safe and no harm will come to you. Take the step forward into the fire. Feel the fire as it removes and transforms and rebirths all that you need it to. You can stay held within the flames, dancing with them, in full expression of yourself and the season of life you are in. Or you can keep walking through the flames. Follow your call, your intuition. (pause for as long as you need or want)

On the other side of the fire, your dreams and desires swirling round within the confines of your inner cauldron are bubbling now. How do you feel? Is there any clarity or change of belief around who or what was altered in the flames? (pause for a breath) Thank the fire for its part in your growth and evolution. It's time to begin your journey back. The fire remains burning to remind you of the fire that is aflame within you.

Start to journey back along the path you travelled earlier. Notice what has changed since your previous journey inwards along the spiral. How does it look? What time of day or night is it? What season are you in now? What do you hear or smell? (pause for a breath)

Notice any thoughts that are popping into your consciousness. Notice too the pace at which you are walking. (pause for as long as it takes to walk the path)

You are back at the threshold now. You know that you can return here at any time to once again walk the spiral path and pass through the flames of transformation. Take a deep breath into your womb space and thank it for keeping safe all you will birth or rebirth into this world. Another deep breath in, into your heart space and thank it for its unconditional love and support for you and all you do. And finally another deep inhale, filling your body and exhale through the soles of your feet, grounding yourself back into the hear and now.

When you are ready, open your eyes.

Welcome back.

Journal Prompts

- What is my relationship/connection with time – is

it cyclic or linear? Why do I hold this opinion?
- How do I use and measure time?
- What calendar system(s) work best for me?
- Do I follow the Wheel of the Year?
- What do the festivals of the Wheel of the Year mean to me and can I find further reason for their purpose in my current life, in sync with my values?
- Do any of the eight festivals hold more significance than others? If so, why? Do any of the eight festivals pass me by as irrelevant? If so, why?
- Do I feel connected or drawn to the moon? If so, is it important? Why?
- Does the lunar cycle have any impact on my life e.g. energetically?
- What rituals if any do I hold sacred in relation to the lunar cycle and why?
- What's my relationship with my period? Do I dread it? Tolerate it? Accept it as part of my monthly routine? Celebrate it? Behold it as sacred?
- Why do I feel the way I do about my cycle?
- How did I experience my first period and how has that shaped my menstrual journey?
- Would I consider honouring my menarche retrospectively?
- How do I feel about the menopausal journey?
- How well do I trust and know my cycle as a barometer to my general health?
- What are my thoughts on menstrual/lunar cycle synchronicity?
- How do I relate to the archetypes representing a woman's life cycle?
- How do I honour my inner Maiden, Mother, Wild Woman, Crone?

- "Mother" - who she is, what does she represent, what is my connection to the word, the emotion, the meaning?
- Who were my role models in my Maiden years? Were they different in my teen years compared to my latter maiden years?
- Who were/are my mother, wild woman, crone role models?
- Why are/were my role models inspiring to me – what qualities, characteristics, values do they possess?
- What lessons am I living with and now appreciating from my life experiences?
- Do I wish the Red Tent had been part of my life when I was a maiden, and remain so now?
- If applicable, would I share in a Red Tent with my daughter if there was one available? Or with my mother?
- What does being an older woman mean to me?
- Who are the wise women in my life? What influence have they had on the elder woman I will become?
- How do I view ageing? Why?
- How do I view death? How do I feel about my own mortality? Why?
- If I could turn back time, would I?
- From the meditation: How did I feel walking the path initially? Why? How did I feel standing at the threshold of the fire? Why? How and what did I experience in the flames? How and did I feel walking the return path? Why?

Action

- Mark in your diary or on your calendar the full and

dark moon dates and notice how you feel on and around these particular days. Journal any experiences and over the course of a few months see if any patterns begin to appear.
- Pick a day, perhaps a weekend and rise with the sun, sleep with the moon – no alarm clock or artificial electric light. Reset your circadian rhythm. See how you feel, notice how you sleep.
- Disregard the Gregorian calendar to live by the lunar cycle, new moon to dark moon.
- Mark in your diary the Wheel of the Year and celebrate each festival in a manner fitting to the celebration and your understanding of it. Record anything you notice about the season, how you feel, emotionally and physically, what is growing in your neighbourhood parks and wild spaces, the weather, what you are drawn to eat, what do you see, hear, smell?
- Write a letter to each of the seasons, sharing what it is you are most looking forward to in each season, what brings you joy in that time, what challenges you face at this time of year, how you live in the season and any reflections or observations you have. Reread your letter when the season comes around again to see how you have grown since the previous cycle, what has changed, been let go of or flourished.
- Track your menstrual cycle for the next 3 months, either in a mandala form, an app on your phone or just in your journal and look for any patterns in energy, mood, weight, habits, etc.
- Write a letter to your Maiden self, Mother self, Wild Woman self and Crone self, either from retrospective point of view or to your future self for that phase. What emotions and feelings are you holding regarding that period, share your expectations,

experiences, wisdoms, forgive yourself if needed. Be free - these are letters to you, not to anyone else.
- Strike up a conversation about death – how you feel about it generally and about your own mortality.
- Plan your funeral – even if it just to pick the music! Share what your preferences are.

THREAD THREE

SHE

***SHE is the Great Mother,
Divine Feminine, Gaia.
She is the earth, the seas,
the weather, the seasons.
She is in us and around us.
She is Maiden, Mother,
Mage & Crone.
She is both healer and
destroyer.
She is protector and warrior.
She is sacred. She is magic.
She is Creatrix.
She is all things;
light and dark.
She is connection.
She is whole.
She is life.***

~ Lissa Corra ~

10

Divine Feminine

Sovereign Holy Eternal
~ Lissa Corra ~

The Divine Feminine, who is She and what does She mean to you?

   I resisted and refused the notion of divine anything for the majority of my life having been an atheist since around 12 years old but more and more over the past few years the feminine aspect kept nudging me. This was not in a religious context and absolutely not in "a woman in the sky watching my every move" like the idea of the Big Man with the white beard, but more that the Goddess is part of everyone, She lives within us and that She is not a separate entity. She is always present, we just need to open up to find her. I am still pondering this though, I don't have an exact answer as to who She is or know what's the truth, I'm just going with my own feelings and interpretation.

We are the embodiment of the Her, the Divine Feminine

The Divine Feminine is known by so many names in so many cultures across the entire planet. She is revered and reflected in various guises and archetypes. She is one essence and She is a multitude of deities each with specific characteristics. Does that contradiction matter?

If you connect with, work with or simply acknowledge Her, you will have your own very specific way to do so, because She will have called you in a way unique to you. If you are starting out and gingerly feeling your way into the feminine divinity, it may seem confusing or complicated with regards to where to start. With that in mind, I will endeavour to introduce Her to you, in her many forms from my perspective and understanding from my heritage and culture; Celtic, predominantly Scots.

Ancient Celtic life is purported to have been matrilineal rather than patriarchal. This does not mean it was the opposite of patriarchy (dominance and superiority of the male over female where the physical feminine and feminine aspects and traits are as treated and considered as inferior) but is of equality between the sexes and was the alleged foundation of Celtic tradition. The purpose was for the collective to come together, work together, a balance of power and sharing of the load. Fertility was viewed as the attractive quality over beauty. The family lineage was through the red thread of the mother line. This was not a hierarchical society, not until the fall of matriarchy towards the end of the Stone Age and the rise of patriarchy in the Metal Ages of bronze and iron. The Celts arrived to the British Isles during the Iron Age. Might they have retained their matrilineal connection for longer here in Britain whilst patriarchy was gaining momentum on the continent? Who knows. Interpret the information we have as you feel is appropriate.

While there are no written records of life at this time, the remains of statues and figurines from the period show reverence for and the evolution of the Goddess with how She was viewed through the ages.

The oldest form of goddess worshipping paraphernalia discovered is the Venus of Willendorf from approx 25,000 years ago. It was unearthed in Austria in 1908.

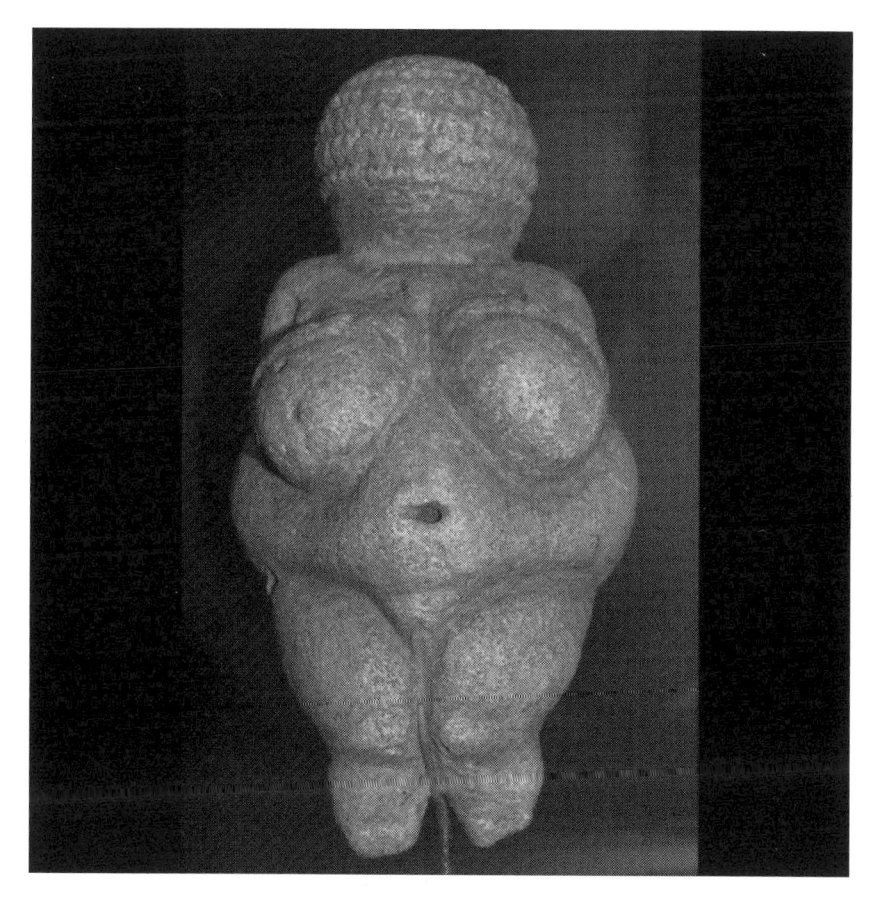

She is a renowned for her voluptuous, ripe and juicy form,

large breasts, full abdomen, and round hips; a symbol of fertility, strength, power and nourishment. She is the Creatrix. There are many statues from the Stone Age that present women with this full, curvaceous figure, focussing on fertility.

With patriarchy's increasing momentum came the steady decline of matriarchy and the reducing presence and perceived importance of woman. The statues then began to show women in significantly more diminutive forms and in restrictive clothing. The desired standard was no longer fertility but beauty, and that standard was determined and driven by men. They set the ideals that women were to aspire to and so we witness the start of comparison culture and woman being measured against one another.

It was during the late Iron Age and into the early centuries of the common era, when the Romans were on their cross continental campaigns that the significant changes in what was deemed "civilised" came into ordinary acceptance. Female sexuality became demonised, the notion being reinforced via the tales of the temptress Eve and the evil actions of Lilith. Men could and did have free sexual liberties to indulge in marital sex, extra-martial sex including with prostitutes and with their slaves as well as enjoy homosexual pleasures. It was legal to be raped by a Roman soldier. This was absolutely not the case for women, and in particular lesbian women. The fear of the feminine grew alongside mistrust; women and the Goddess became an easy scapegoat for all ills and ails.

The Goddess and feminine deities were removed or reduced. Many Scottish local deities are long forgotten or have been reframed as faery queens instead. By excluding woman from spirituality and esoteric teachings, the mono male god took up residence and became the almighty. Previously the Goddess had a consort, her mate, the Divine Masculine who was her equal, they complemented one another, but that was no longer the case. The myths, gospels and sacred texts were all written by men for men and suppressed the feminine, which was considered to be lowly, emotionally and physically weak, deceitful, subservient and whose menstruations were dirty. The family lineage now followed the paternal lineage through through the white thread of the father's father's father.

Nevertheless, She persisted.

The stories, myths and legends remained but were carefully hidden yet were told and retold time over time. After two millennia She is re-emerging, women are reconnecting with her and rising all across the globe. She lives on in many names from Isis, Inanna, Pele, Saraswati, Athena, Kali Ma, Kuan Yin, Mawu, Mother Mary, Diana, Mary Magdalene, Yemanya, Ixchel, Freya, Frigg, Vesta, White Buffalo Woman and many, many, many more.

For the purposes of this book and from my own path and connection, I am going to share the Divine Feminine of Celtic Britain. When I began exploring the Divine Feminine, I did deliberately seek out and explore Celtic Goddesses in my quest to find, actually I don't know what I initially hoped to find or for why, just something that made sense to me.

Who is She of these lands then? The origins of some deities cannot be said to be native to Britain or of Celtic heritage as the written history came via the Romans, who brought with them their own deities. Some Roman deities were aligned with She who was already here, such as Sulis, who became known as Sulis Minerva (Minerva being a Roman goddess of wisdom). I have not listed every possible deity just some, pertaining to the island of Great Britain; Scotland, Wales, England. I have not included Irish deities unless She was found on this island too. Ireland is a different island and for the most part, a different country which has retained a rich and healthy account of her Goddesses. So with that in mind, who was and is revered on this land:

Andraste – Goddess of War and was called upon by Boudicca, the Celtic Iceni Tribe Warrior Queen when charging into battle. (Eng)
Arianrhod – Triple Goddess, Mother aspect. Goddess of fertility and reincarnation. Her name means Silver Wheel. (Wal)
Blodeuwedd – Triple Goddess, Maiden Aspect. Goddess of initiation, emotions and spring flowers. Her name mean Flower Face. (Wal)
Boderia – Matron goddess of the River Forth, meaning Deaf or Soundless One. (Sco)
Branwen - Goddess of love and means White Raven. (Wal)
Brigit/Bride/Brigid – Triple Goddess, Maiden aspect. Goddess of fire, smithcraft, the hearth, healing, poetry, arts and crafts and learning. Associated with Imbolg. (Sco, Wal, Ire)
Cailleach – Triple Goddess, Crone Aspect. The Queen of Winter, destruction and death. (Sco, Ire)
Cerridwen - Goddess of transformation, rebirth and knowledge. The most powerful witch/sorceress in Celtic lore. Her name means cauldron. (Wal)
Clota/Clutha – Matron Goddess of the River Clyde meaning the Purifying One. (Sco)
Corra – Goddess of transformation, prophesy, the connection to the underworld. Often shape shifting into a crane. (Sco)
Coventina – Powerful river Goddess, probably Roman in origin. She has shrines dedicated to her along Hadrian's Wall. (Eng, Sco)

Elen (of the Ways) – The antlered goddess. She tracked the ways, the paths, through the land. She is wild and young and found in woodlands. (British, probably Welsh)
Epona - Goddess of horses. (Britain)
Great Mother – Known also as The Lady. Goddess of fertility, creation, the earth. (Britain)
Gyre Carlin – Also known as Nicnevin, a Goddess of Samhuinn, magic, protection and divination. She is a crone and fierce. (Sco)
Momu – Goddess of the earth, caves, lochs and wells, but more especially hillsides and mountains. (Sco)
Nemetona – Goddess of sacred groves and spaces. (Eng)
Queen of Elphame – She is also known as Nicnevin, the Queen of Faeries and Spirits, goddess of death and disease and the head of the Unseelie Court, malevolent in nature. (Sco)
Rhiannon – Goddess of horses, artistry and magic. She was Queen of the Fae. (Wal)
Scáthach – Warrior Goddess and destroyer. Patroness of martial arts and known as The Shadow. (Sco)
Sulis – Mother Goddess of sacred water, hot springs and healing. (Eng)
Tava/Tatha – Matroness Goddess of the River Tay meaning Silent One. (Sco)

The Goddess was found in nature, in all living things. She was honoured, celebrated and prayed to, offerings and sacrifices made to her and in her honour. Some Goddesses are seasonal or are called upon to aid in a particular area of life. The use of Goddess Archetypes is helpful in doing this, to assist channelling the energy required. In Celtic spirituality the Goddess is regarded as a Triple Aspect form as the Maiden, Mother, Crone and there are various deities who take up the mantle for each phase, such as Bride the Maiden, Cerridwen the Mother and Cailleach the Crone. It is believed that the the Triple Goddess was the foremother of the Holy Trinity; the Father, Son and Holy Spirit.

11

Modern Spirituality

Less love 'n' light more real 'n' raw
~ Lissa Corra ~

Spirituality. What does it mean? Seriously! What does it mean to be 'spiritual'?

The Cambridge Dictionary defines spirituality as:

- *relating to deep feelings and beliefs, especially religious beliefs*

and the Free Dictionary states that Spiritual means:

- *concerned with sacred or religious things; refined; sensitive*

I think, in modern parlance, 'spirituality' means different things to different people; it means whatever you understand it to be, in relation to your personal belief set.

Spirituality has become one of those terms used and, at times, over used and not always with clarity, but rather an air of mystique or pretension. There is an element of wankery attached to the word as it is banded about to express one's enlightened state of being. But it is also a sincere description of what some people experience or believe whether instead of, or alongside, their religion. Is that any clearer? I'm not actually convinced that it is.

I had a friend tell me many years ago that neither she nor her husband were religious people, but that they were spiritual. I remember being somewhat perplexed at the time but not wanting to look ignorant, I just accepted the statement. Only in the past 4 or 5 years have I given the word any pause for thought. It hadn't ever been part of my consciousness when considering my path and beliefs until I started hearing and seeing it used more and more on social media, where it is the height of fashion.

From a personal perspective, I do not consider myself 'religious' (I was christened as a baby into the *Church of Scotland*, but at eight weeks old, that choice was not mine to make. I have never felt any affinity with the church and haven't attended a service other than for hatches, matches or dispatches since I left school). I don't believe in God the Almighty, the mono God of creation. I can accept that Jesus was a real man but that his miracles were more symbolic rather than literal. I don't believe in heaven and hell other than that they were man-made constructs created to instil fear, compliance and obedience. I do however believe that we are all part of something greater than just this existence on this one planet. There has to be life elsewhere, space is infinite! We cannot possibly be the only creatures. I also believe in energy, ghosts, reincarnation and that we are souls inhabiting a human body. Oh and I celebrate Christmas and Easter as they are a time with and for family, but they're very much cultural and traditional not religious observances. Obviously these are just my beliefs and am in no way suggesting that yours ought to be the same.

Since high school I have identified as atheist, although at a guess I would say that that 2001 census has me down as Presbyterian Christian, Church of Scotland, as I still lived with my parents and they completed the form. However in the 2011 census I listed my religious beliefs as Pagan.

Despite being born in the "new age" (the term which came in to being during the 1970s), I am an old soul with a knowing of the old ways, as in the old pre-Christian ways. As result I am a bit of a mash up of the old and new.

What do I mean by "the old ways"? What does "new age" mean? When I think of the Old Ways, I think of the pre-Christian times, in the matriarchal goddess worshipping times. When Nature ruled. A simpler time in terms of what was required to be done, how people went about their lives, meeting their needs individually and collectively for the family and community. A small yet hard life, living off the land and at the mercy of the elements, and their understanding and observations of the natural world for which they were a part of. A time when changing seasons were recognised by experiencing the seasons themselves rather than by a fixed calendar. Honouring revered deities or the Mother Goddess with love rather than fear. The village mentality and way of life, living in sync with the cycles of nature speaks to me of the old ways. The people were of the land. This is merely my interpretation, yours may be completely different.

Contrast this with the New Age and my inner feeling changes from slow, steady and at peace, to a buzz of energy and a feeling of "whoosh", psychedolic madness and woo-woo. What comes immediately to my mind upon hearing New Age is a plethora of images and labels: new-age-hippie-dippy-claptrap, crystals, The West, burning sage, cultural appropriation, ancestry, the universe, energy, chakras,

Cacao Ceremony, Bali, retreats, coconut oil, essential oil, meditation, yoga, yoni, homeopathy, love'n'light, spiritual bypass, the moon, light workers, peace man, tarot cards, a goddess for everything from all parts of the globe, free spirit, earthing, grounding, vegan, the list goes on, feel free to insert your own interpretations. Some of it is ancient in origin but is part of the New Age scene. Some of it makes me uncomfortable, some of it is given a cursory eye-roll and other bits I really connect with and practice regularly.

So why do I think I have an old soul and a knowing of the old ways? And how do I marry that remembering with the new fangled new age? I feel a very real connection to both the history and geography of the island in which I live. For instance, I have an unexplained physical reaction to the city of Edinburgh when I am there. I have never lived there. Years ago I worked in Wales, and when I came home every other weekend, my train would have me arrive at Haymarket Station, Edinburgh, to then get my connection for the last 30 miles home. Standing on that platform, breathing in the smell of hops on a cold autumnal evening, I always felt "I'm home". Any and every night out in Edinburgh over the years always felt like home - I feel safe in this city yet never have the same feelings or notions in Glasgow or any other city I've visited. Similarly to the the village I live in now; I had no connection to it prior to moving but once we moved I immediately felt that this is where I belong and felt settled here, I love the land the feeling it evokes in me. I certainly never felt even a smidge of that contentedness in my previous home in which I lived for 12 years. I have always been fascinated with herbs and herbal healing (not really done anything with this fascination other than making teas from the herbs I planted and grew, but its always been there), been curious about the moon, the changing seasons, and witchcraft (I'm a life long lover of all things witchy). Once I started tracing my family tree (I went back to my 4th Great Grandmother in my Mother's line) much of what I discovered about my family makes so much sense to the person I am and the interests I have long held. The reading, research and practice I have been actively seeking and learning from over the years have revealed many "YES" moments and an awakening of things I already knew, deep down, coupled with an insatiable thirst for more knowledge.

We are waking and remembering; the old ways, the forgotten skills, the stories, herstory.
Remember. Reclaim. Rise.

Combining these base feelings and knowings/rememberings with the modern world has been for the most part fairly straight forward with a few stumbles along the way. I have real issues around cultural appropriation and people claiming indigenous ritual or ceremony for their own when they have no connection to that culture, perhaps save for an ancestry DNA test that identified 1% trendy ethnicity. Many cultures, including my own, have been through years of persecution and oppression, some to the point of being classed as criminal. I truly believe that our own cultures where we live or have grown up are rich in their own history, traditions, folklore and language that cherry picking the cool rituals, tools and symbology (which, in the spiritual spheres, is rife) from another's is not OK. It would appear that this is perfectly acceptable if the practice is then referred to as eclectic...

This then throws up more questions such as where is the line between appropriation and appreciation? The world has become a melting pot of traditions and blended ways; a global village of sorts. Or is that just the wash that's been applied to cover cultural appropriation? The point here is not to lecture, preach, judge or dictate what anyone else should be or not be doing or how one ought to practice, or what and who to believe in, but more to invite you to question *what* you do, *why* you do it, *where* it comes from, and *what* your connection is. Challenge yourself to understand where your spiritual journey began and where it is going.

Every culture has its own myths and legends, rituals and ceremonies just waiting to be remembered, reclaimed, embraced, lived and loved deeply.

If you have no spiritual path, what is your reasoning there? When did you last give it any consideration? Perhaps it doesn't need looked at, but I suggest that perhaps it may, even if just to blow off the dust on long held beliefs and opinions.

During the first lock down last year I certainly dusted off the cobwebs of my whys and hows of my practice. I found that the online spiritual space was overwhelming. I needed to switch it off and break free from its dense, saturated opinions and competing voices. In my journal I wrote:

"The path upon which I walk has become congested, crowded and polluted. No longer can I see the beauty, hear the call or feel the truth of what I'm doing or where I'm going. I feel suffocated, stifled and thoroughly exhausted. Where am I? I am being swallowed up by the ravenous appetite of the collective, seasoned to suit the common and popular taste. I am a diluted version of myself and my truth. Do I continue along this muddy, mobbed and potholed way or veer off here and navigate my own way; reclaim my own journey and reconnect with my north

star?"

As fashions come and go, the current trend for *spirituality* and the blending of hippie / gypsy / bohemian / pagan (all of which are completely different and not at all synonymous with one another) looks like it's here to stay for quite some time yet. And as interest and popularity in all things witchy and spiritual soars, so too does the dogma. Yet this is not a dogmatic path! Not only was I feeling bombarded by the constant information overload and the saccharine infused frilly adjectives of the spiritual lexicon, but I was also contributing to the noise with my own words.

I had become fairly fluent in the floofiness of this tongue with its distinct air of being otherworldly, serene and/or mystical, but always "of the light". In the cold light of day however, this is a style of language which now sounds, to my ear, insincere, pretentious and not how folk talk in regular conversation. In the end all I wanted to say was SHUT UP! It's too much!

Taking myself off of social media and getting outside as often as possible to sit or work in my garden with my hands in the earth, walk the local woods, letting my bare feet touch the earth or grass has been the most simple and effective way to reconnect. Following the lunar cycle, the seasons and my own cycle keep me grounded and in tune with myself and my spiritual practice during these tumultuous times we live in. And it is enough.

I am of this land, of this place, in the modern "new age" whilst reconnecting to, remembering and honouring the old ways. Is it the best of both? I think so, but as with all things learning, growing and evolving, nothing is certain, including my opinion.

Regardless of whether you are of the old ways or the new age or a blend of both or on your own innate spiritual journey, what you are doing is reclaiming feminine spirituality. Taking back ownership and power of a practice that is meaningful and connected *to you*, that understands you and your being, in body and soul. The times are changing and the doors are being blown off the broom closet as more and more women are stepping out, owning and identify with either or both of the titles Witch or Priestess. Without fear.

You may wonder, are they the same or different? What are the differences? Can you be both? (Yes, I believe you can). Certainly, they both require a calling of sorts. You don't wake up one day and decide I'm a Witch or I'm a Priestess. Both take dedication and work to learn the teachings; from books and actual life, from cycling with nature again and again, season after season, year after year. There is no end point, it's a continual path of learning, evolution, experimentation, mishap, mistakes, unlearning, intuition, blood, tears, loss, joy, grace, understanding, confusion, soul deep exploration, rejection, connection, unearthing, grounding, discovering and listening. It's ownership of, and a choice to pursue, this path. And that is just scratching the surface. All the while carrying on with the day job.

Both Priestesses and Witches work with rituals, sacred days, times and seasons. Some may cast circles before commencing rituals or work, some may not. Both understand the nature of balance and the cycle of life. Important point to note is that here is no devil worship in either case.

What is a Witch?
We all know what a witch is, right? The Oxford Dictionary defines a witch as:

- *a woman thought to have magic powers, especially evil ones, popularly depicted as wearing a black cloak and pointed hat and flying on a broomstick.*

and Merriam Webster recognises her as:

- *one that is credited with usually malignant supernatural powers especially: a woman practising usually black witchcraft often with the aid of a devil or familiar.*

Yes, evil, magical hags not to be trusted, rather than wise women with skills and knowledge in the healing arts, midwifery or in gardening. Patriarchy and the church did a sterling job demonising women they saw as a threat and persecuting many innocent people, mainly women, for "crimes" they did not commit. We all know of the Salem Witch Trials of 1692-93 in Massachusetts, where 200 people were accused and 20 people executed as witches. In Scotland, our shameful history is far greater with 4,000-6,000 accusations and 1500 **recorded** executions during the burning times of the Witch Trials. The Scottish numbers were 5 times higher than the rest of Europe, such was the pure hatred and fear fuelled by the kirk.

A witch by my definition is:

- *a woman (or man) who is in service to no-one unless she chooses to be and who practices witchcraft*

It is a craft like any other and has to be practiced and developed over time. The craft can include an array of specialisations from divination, spell work, herb and plant work to intuitive guidance, life coaching and healing via complimentary or traditional medicine. It is not an exhaustive list, just like the list of types of witches is not exhaustive either. The main types of Witches are (in no particular order): solitary, garden, kitchen, moon/lunar, Pagan, Wiccan, coven, hedge, hereditary, green, traditional, faery, sea, grey, elemental, crystal, eclectic, hearth, weather, energy, artist, magical, forest, urban, healing, spiritual, nature, new/apprentice and new-age. I have probably left our more types than I can remember.

To be a witch does not automatically mean she is Wiccan or Pagan. Not all witches are Wiccan, not all Pagans are witches!

Unless a witch is part of a coven, there is no formal training that has to be completed before being able to call oneself a witch. It is not a title that one ought to take lightly however. There are courses a plenty online for how to be or how to practice, but getting outside and attuning to nature is as worthy a teacher as any course. Books and blogs for guidance are helpful but not vital. The costumery of witchcraft is not necessary either - wear a hat or cloak, don't wear a hat or cloak, have a broom, don't have a broom, have a black cat, don't have a black cat (have a dog or a gold fish or a chicken or no pets because allergies - it doesn't matter!) Fun yes, necessary no.

The word Witch is a powerful one that when I hear it, still makes me a little uneasy, despite my life long love of "witches". This is in part due to perception, the old fears and hatred of witches deliberately driven by the kirk have been replaced with ridicule and derision by the general populous. In the modern world where, for the most part, the fear of being burnt at the stake is a thing of the past, caution is still exercised when discussing the hidden world of witches and priestesses in certain company as much of the foregone stigma heavily attached to either word, though predominantly on the witch word, remains. The witch wound is deep!

"There is a little witch in all of us"
~ Aunt Jet, Practical Magic ~

What is a Priestess?
According to the Oxford English Dictionary she is:

- *a female priest of a non-Christian religion.*

Merriam Webster Dictionary defines a Priestess as:

- *a woman authorized to perform the sacred rites of a religion and*
- *a woman regarded as a leader (of a movement)*

My own meaning of what a Priestess is, can be described as but not restricted to:

- *a woman in service to those who need her (her community) and to the Great Mother, Divine Feminine.*

She has usually undertaken some formal training. Training in counselling and spiritual coaching has to be learned properly and will cost. There are many different types of Priestess too: high, initiated, earth, shamanic, women's spiritual leader, oracle, medicine woman, ritual leader, ceremonial leader, wise one, ancient, modern-day, in-training, celebrant and more.

Ancient Priestesses across the globe in matriarchal societies prayed to and were devoted to the Great Mother They were revered by their communities for their wisdom, their experience, their leadership and their connection to the Divine. They lived by nature's cycles and performed and facilitated rites and rituals. They both lead and served.

Modern day Priestesses are reclaiming and remembering the Goddess, bringing back the understood or interpreted ancient teachings as best they can and making them relevant to modern times. A Priestess today is not living in seclusion on an isle shrouded in mists (although that does sound immensely appealing), she could be your kid's teacher, the checkout operator at the supermarket, your hairdresser or accountant! There is an association with the role of the Priestess that she must be holier-than-thou in that nice / lovely / glittery / good-girl bubble of sweetness in a flower crown, when in fact she may be hated or distrusted because the woman has unshakable boundaries. A Priestess is compassionate, respectful and strong *because* of her boundaries.

Regardless of the time, a Priestess is continually doing the work, exploring the depths of herself and who she is in order to serve the Goddess, be it Gaia, The Great Mother, or any number of deities from the world over, from any number of pantheons or the Goddess that resides within all, as well as both serving and leading her community.

As a Ceremonial Priestess my role is in service to women who gather in my circles, guiding and priestessing them through rites of passage ceremonies and rituals. I honour and revere the Divine Feminine, as the Great Mother, encompassing all her aspects, channelling her energy as required.

By stoking the fires of the mysteries, protecting and remembering who we are I invite you to reclaim your soul truth and essence, igniting the spark of curiosity to aid you on your spiritual journey to yourself and perhaps, if you are drawn, to divinity within.

12

Connection

***We are all connected;
experiences, relationships and
lifetimes woven together
throughout the fabric of time.
Find the thread.***
~Lissa Corra ~

In spiritual chat there is much said about connection, but connection to what or to whom? To Her, to each other, the nature, to the seasons, to the moon, to ourselves? Yes, to all of it or just some of it! But not to none of it, we must have a connection to ourselves. The knowing of our who, our what and our why.

The thread of connection weaves its way between us and amongst us, through the ages from the start of time and will continue onwards. We are connected to our roots and to wherever our branches reach. Connection. Nothing superficial but connection on a real level, with raw truths and authenticity of who we are behind our public persona. Do you feel connected?

Being in the global lock down provided me with the gift of space and time to sort myself out and to re-establish my connection to myself and my practice. Connecting the dots so to speak to my ancestors, to nature, to the genus loci (spirit of place i.e. your neighbourhood, local area), to myself, to Her. We, as the general populous, have become so disconnected, perhaps feeling cut off from our roots and from nature, and in this pandemic, from each other. (Video calls are not my idea of a good time.)

> ***Connection;***
> ***to the land,***
> ***to the ancestors,***
> ***to each other.***
> ***To the present.***
> ***Truth. Honesty.***
> ***No masks. No hiding.***
> ***Connection.***

In the awakening of your inner Wild, to what or to whom do you want to connect with? Is it your ancestors? A commitment to a dedicated spiritual practice? To the Divine Feminine herself or an associated archetype or deity? To the land? To the seasons? To the sky? To your intuition and own spiritual growth? To magic and your own intrinsic power? To *something*, but you don't know what that is, other than a feeling? And importantly, why? I can't answer your why, that is for you to figure out, but I can perhaps offer somewhere to start with regards your what.

First of all this may seem like a daunting task, a huge undertaking. I mean, where does one start in this maze of paths with more branches than the Fortingall Yew (before tourists started lopping them off as souvenirs)? I am going to suggest that simplicity is the nature of the beast here; stripped back to the bones and start gently. We have already looked at the seasons, the moon, your own inner cycles, and an introduction to Her, so you have a basis for further exploration, practice and ritual if you are drawn in those directions. I encourage you to solidify that foundational knowledge before building on it and swamping it with more information gleaned from a plethora of different sources. To do so you learn through living with and observing the earthly and lunar seasons through their cycles and keeping your own notes, therefore creating your own personal connection. This is truly intimate work. The more you live it, breathe it and experience it with your own senses, the deeper your connection, the stronger your power and intuition, and more profound your wisdoms will be. You are creating a touchstone in life that will provide you with a content way of being and a practice that is meaningful, is important and sacred *to you*, one that brings joy and comfort and honours *your* sovereignty.

Let us look at 21st century connection...to stuff! Specifically what you need before you start, and for use during, to be able to have a spiritual practice of any sort. Got your shopping list and pencil ready? Let's go!

But first, let me ask you, do you believe in magic? You don't have to; it is all around you. YOU are magic. Do you believe me?

> **"Well there's magic all around you,**
> **if I do say so myself."**
> ~ *Stevie Nicks* ~

All around us we are told we need to do this or have that in order to "make magic" (whatever that means to you). The internet and some chain stores have caught on to the current trend for all things witchcraft, paganism, spirituality, and a hotch potch of all things appropriated from oppressed cultures, where you can buy all manner of accoutrements and paraphernalia to "do it right".

When did it all get so complicated and prescribed? In the capitalist age, the next big thing is always on the horizon. Some fads come and go with their one minute of fame while others have the longevity. Right now, the New Age is in vogue. And there is a crap tonne of money to be made. Money is magic, right? Nope! Shop or online bought magic isn't YOUR magic. In my humble opinion:

we need to simplify spirituality and rewild magic not commercialise it.

Do we need to buy that specific crystal because it holds a particular energy? Do we need to buy that bunch of flowers with the right significant meaning or candle in the appropriate colour? Does that spell kit with the candle and the "smudge stick" (stolen from Native American heritage) and the prescribed "spell" have more power than the words spelled, written or spoken, by the person setting those intentions, which are imbued with their own energy and feelings? The answer is of course, No. You don't need anything other than yourself and your intentions. If you like and need stuff, consider what you already have at home, in the garden or little trinkets you've picked up on nature walks that 'spoke' to you. Are they less valuable or significant because they weren't purchased or deemed "correct"? Which leads me on to correspondences.

There are prescribed correspondences for EVERYTHING! Certain colours, crystals, essential oils, incense, candles, ribbons, herbs, flowers, foods, animals, times of the day, days of the week, seasons, numbers, weather conditions, elements, trees, lunar phases, astrological placement of the planets, etc that NEED to be adhered to for "magic" to work, to do it right. Bollocks to that!

Magic has been caught and caged for capitalism.

To need most of this stuff means to buy it. But do you know what you can't buy? Intuition. You cannot buy intuition because, that, my friend, is not for sale! And nothing is more potent than trusting personal intuition; it's the most valuable tool you have at your disposal. It needs to be worked and exercised and above all, trusted and listened to. Everything else is fluff and fun.

Don't get me wrong, I enjoy a bit of fluff and fun - of course I have a cauldron! Yes, I divine using tarot and oracle decks. All I am saying is that we don't *need* it. Do I think our ancestors needed to have the right correspondences to work? Nope, I believe they used what they had, a cauldron was an actual cooking receptacle, and they followed their intuition. No need to over complicate matters for what is essentially the essence of the New Age; social media and our audience. That is not real. There is absolutely no need to part with any cash to have the "right" gear, none at all, it's all the glamour of aesthetics (and clever marketing). Unless the glamorous aesthetic is part of the connection for you, in which case shop until your heart is content. This is your story, your practice and your connection after all.

When starting out or exploring a different path, you may find what others have done to be a useful insight to what may work for them. I will always recommend reading books, books and more books, but above all, please remember to trust yourself, write up and read/reread your own notes and observations, question everything and keep it simple.

Controversially, I'm going to throw crystals in to the connection mix. How do we meld reverence for Mother Earth and the multi billion dollar/pound industry that crystals have become? I have a very small collection of crystals, most of which were gifted to me. They are beautiful but I don't use them for anything other than decoration or jewellery (I wear moonstones in my necklace). However, crystals have always tugged at me ethically. They are so very pretty. Every spiritual person worth her salt has more crystals than Imelda Marcos has shoes but the truth is they are simply not sustainable.

The blood diamonds of the spiritual world
~ Eva Wiseman, The Guardian, 16th June 2019 ~

Crystals have to be mined (more often than not in countries with questionable human rights laws. If they don't give a stuff about humans, then environmental care is way down that priority list) and mining is not environmentally friendly in any way. So in protecting and revering The Great Mother, I no longer purchase crystals no matter how ethical the supplier claims to be. The crystals I do have I will keep (there are three I will never part with, two of which were given to me for my 30th by an old friend that were hers to begin with, and a labradorite pebble that I adore and just feels good in my hand, I can't explain it, but I love it) or will gift onwards to someone who will appreciate and use them. Do you have a connection to crystals? Where do you stand with ethics versus desire and connection?

Confession: I do have to admit though, that there is a jeweller on Instagram I follow and she has theee most beautiful goddess rings she has created using silver, moonstone and labradorite (could there be a more gorgeous combo?? I think not!). I would be lying if I said I didn't want one...like really want one!!

Next up is a place in which to plug in to your connection. Creating an altar space can be enormously useful to you on your spiritual journey, and it can be as simple or as elaborate as you please. An altar is simply a dedicated place where you can sit and focus your attention or energy and connect into your practice, be that in meditation, prayer, working intentions or manifestations, journaling, divining or any activity you are involved in. Altars can be a solitary candle on a window sill to a shelf or table with ornaments and trinkets, leaves, flowers, feathers, crystals or anything you connect with to represent you, the elements, the ancestors, the Goddess, the season, the lunar phase, or again, anything that you are called to hold in sacred space. At this moment in time I have no set altar; I am the altar myself as identified in the chant:

Earth my body, water my blood, Air my breath and fire my spirit.

But when I hold circle or ceremony for other people, I absolutely create a specific altar for the occasion. It is a central point for all concerned and it brings everyone together.

Magic; it needs to be felt, to be released, to be rewilded.

Mixing my practice up and going with what I'm feeling and called to do instead of set rituals, including self created and self imposed ones, has been a form of rewilding my own magic and simplifying my spirituality. I don't live my path to only pick it up to perform rituals at particular lunar phases with all sorts of paraphernalia. I just need myself, my intuition, my connection and living it daily. Magic is already in me, in you, in us; in all our uniqueness.

Over the many years I have been walking this path I have tried various ways of doing and shoe-horning other people's way into my way trying to make it work, it's very much been trial and error. The reverse is equally true; I actively denied and resisted the Divine Feminine for a number of years as I previously mentioned, but then I found I couldn't any longer and so now She is part of my practice. What I have come to realise and appreciate is that when something is presented to me and it doesn't fit, it doesn't get to stay, and, as I grow and learn and explore, if something no longer fits, it is released to leave space for what does and can flourish. William Morris' famous quote:

"Have nothing in your home that you do not know to be useful, or believe to be beautiful."

is very relevant here and therefore my cauldron stays, it being both beautiful and useful, and fun too!

I prefer to go with my feelings and mood at any particular time rather than what someone else has decreed as the right way or right "correspondence". For example, let's take smoke cleansing, specifically white sage and Palo Santo. I have used both in the past but haven't used either in personal practice for about three years. Why? I actually hate the smell of white sage, it chokes me rather than cleanses me and Palo Santo gives me a headache. But more importantly, both of these tools are sacred to indigenous cultures of colonised lands and their spiritual rites, plus they are both unsustainable and are on the the endangered lists. Retailers stating that they come from sustainable/ethical sources is a fallacy as they don't exist. I have taken part in rituals and ceremony where white sage has been used and, because I'm polite and have a lifetime of people pleasing tendencies, I have tolerated it but in respect for the practices of those to whom they belong, and to honour myself, I now say no. I do not want to be included in the cleansing. Instead I prefer to use drumming or, for smoke cleansing (saining), incense or the smoke from a fire. There are so many ways to cleanse a person or space without white sage or Palo Santo, such as fresh air or water or salt or sound etc.

Symbolism is a personal connection to how you interpret the meaning or feeling attached to that which you are working with or on.

Language is another important aspect of my connection to my practice. Words have meaning and power, not only to ourselves as individuals but to others too.

When connecting to yourself, there is much to say about intuition. But how do you discern what is intuition and what is fear or ego? How do you know how to trust that what you are feeling is the "right thing" to do? I believe it comes down to how something *feels* in your body. I hold my intuition and knowing of myself in my upper abdominal region, known to many as the solar plexus and heart chakras. Yes it's a cliché but with 20 odd years of stomach related health issues, my gut is well honed in the art of intuition; if something makes me ill or causes me pain, then it's a firm no! My head, heart and womb are the three stations of my operation. Everything I am and do are grounded within these points in me; my wisdoms, intuition and creativity. I don't subscribe to the seven (or nine or twelve) energy chakra systems. I don't have a third eye. And that is okay by me. That's not to say I haven't tried to connect with the chakras, I've even had them re-aligned (which was a beautifully relaxing experience) but it is not part of my practice. It may very well be part of yours, which is great. Explore it and see how you connect with your own body, how you relate to and understand what your body is telling you. *Feel* your way to knowing your intuition and gradually build up the trust.

When considering the feeling of connection, your body is your home; she is the home of your inner Wild, your inner shadow, your soul, your everything. The connection is coming home to yourself and where you feel that strength of self in your body. Feeling comfortable in your own skin, in expressing your emotions, without the need to be comforted by others, in acceptance of who you are, who you were (because you can't change that) and who you will become. It is courageous to connect with your sovereignty and live life in your full, whole, authentic, connected self.

To connect with the Divine Feminine is to know that She is within you always. How She appears and connects with you however, may take many forms, whether She is the Triple Aspect Goddess, or a singular deity, She may appear in your dreams or meditation, or perhaps in nature as an animal such as a deer, or hare or bird. She may be the wind, the sea or the moon, or simply come through your intuition. Only you will know. Only you can interpret what the meaning behind your connection is. Take your time, sit with your experience(s), journal or drum or meditate or dance with the thoughts you have and the internal chat you are having. What guidance are you receiving? What messages are you getting? Don't be disillusioned or disheartened if you get nothing to begin with, listen to your thoughts, notice little synchronicities and nudges, repeating patterns, names or symbols. It takes practice and there are no rules, right way or wrong way or timescales. Just you and your connection, in which ever shape that takes.

In my experience, up until about 4 years ago, Divine anything was a turn off for this Pagan atheist. I also had (have) little to no reverence for the church and its teachings. Yet I repeatedly found myself drawn to Lilith and her story. I feel a connection to who Lilith is/was, a want to reclaim her story and retell it appropriately, not from the patriarchal view with their slander spouted forth as gospel. This is the case for many modern day women. Others are drawn instinctively to Mary Magdalene or Mother Mary. Not necessarily Christian women, but women with a connection to these stories, the untold stories and what Lilith, Mary Magdalene, Mother Mary represent. Recently I was in conversation with a fellow Priestess, where we were discussing the Triple Goddess. In her own personal practice she does not connect with the triple aspect archetype at all, but instead works with Bride the Maiden and Cailleach the Crone energies and archerypes, and the Mother is everpresent in Mother Nature, Earth herself. I have to say I hadn't considered this before but it made perfect sense to me and is now something I am working with in how I view my own practice and connection. See how nothing is set in stone and continues to evolve and shift as our own experience and understandings change and grow? I have adhered to and been in alignment with the four phases of Maiden, Mother, Wild Woman, Crone for so long that rethinking this is challenging yet exciting for me.

Connection to our ancestors means honouring our loved ones to keep their memory alive. We are each here today because of those who have gone before us in both the recent and distant past.

I have clear, fond memories of my maternal grandfather but none of my maternal grandmother who passed when I was a toddler, yet the older I get, the more connected to her I feel and the more I want to learn about her. The stories from my own mother about hers suggests that my Gran was quite a woman, and one I wish I had known. My paternal grandfather died before I was born and my paternal grandmother also passed when I was young (I was five) but by Goddess I remember her and remember her well; even the smell of her teapot, mirrored compact and cigarette pouch. The love I had and still have for her is fierce and I treasure her wedding ring which I have worn since I was fourteen. Despite all their early deaths, I feel connected to each of them, particularly my Papa, who I believe has been with me since birth (he certainly pops up at every spiritualist medium I have visited and has appeared to me in meditation) which gives me great comfort. My connection to my white thread lineage (father line) is strong.

But what about the ancestors that go way back, to time before the living memories of our oldest relatives today? How can we connect to them? If you want to "know" them, a beautiful way to honour your ancestry is to trace it, see where your lineage lies and from whom. Embrace your roots and learn your heritage. You may end up surprised or it may lead to conversations with relatives you've lost contact with and sharing of yet more stories or old photos, with names and people and places, following the crumbs, pieced together by census records and gravestones, national library archives and contacting distant relations. It is a lot of work and it may not provide you with the answers you seek or reveal more than you bargained for, for good or otherwise. Depending on what you find you may not want to "connect" with your ancestors at all! We are connected to them through the treads of time, whether they be someone you want to honour and love or are ashamed or embarrassed by. What ever wonders or horrors they lived through or were involved in, whether they were "good people" but "of their time", whether their beliefs and values reflect ours or not, which ever path they walked, how they lived, loved and breathed, we are here today thanks to them. It is important to remember that you are not them, you come from their stock but you are you independent of the past. It is also not the only way to connect however.

Family trees are not compulsory or even a possibility for many. You can connect in your heart and through meditation and prayer. Wearing their jewellery or having heirlooms in your home is a connection, creating space at your table (called a dumb supper) at celebratory meals to include your ancestors is a connection, visiting the towns or countries where they lived, visiting their grave or by some other means of remembrance, such as burning rosemary, are all ways you can connect with your ancestors, keeping them relevant in the now and carrying them forth into the future. We don't need to know their names to know that the invisible thread of our lineages goes back through time to the first ancestors.

This also makes me think about the future, we are the ancestors of tomorrow; what is (y)our legacy? What kind of ancestor will you become, how will you be remembered and by whom?

To bridge the connection to each other I am (of course) going to drop Circles in here. The next Thread is all about Circles, the how and the why, so will not say anything more on that just now.

Regardless of to whom we make a connection, it is good manners and practice to make an offering in gratitude. That may mean leaving a glass of water or wine out on your altar (obviously it won't be drunk, but is instead an energetic exchange and an acknowledgement of your thanks) or poured onto the earth (known as a libation). An offering of seeds or nuts is appropriate too, as they are absorbed back into the earth through decomposition, or in the the form of nourishment to small mammals or birds.

Personal spiritual practice is not a prescription nor does it have a check list of all the things you have to do, tune into or such. I don't follow expected or assumed leanings or belief systems that don't resonate with me or that I don't connect with or have any connection to. I'm a big believer in knowing ourselves for who we are and following what is true to us individually. Popular or not. And that takes practice.

13

Remember Reconnect Reclaim

Meditation

Meeting HER

Standing, feet hip width apart, eyes closed. Take a deep, womb deep breath and exhale out through the tips of your fingers and down through the soles of your feet. Pause, and repeat for two more breaths.

Now imagine you are in the wild. Where are you? On a hilltop? By the sea? In a forest, the desert or urban jungle? Take another deep breath in, drawing in the energy of the environment around you. Check in with how your feel; what do you see, hear and smell? (pause for a breath) Take a walk, absorb your surroundings. (pause for as long as you need)

You feel at home in this wild. Safe. Alive.

A mist starts to descend and swirl around you in shades of lilac, purple and indigo. You become completely enveloped in the mists. Notice how you feel, how the mists feel as they gather all around you; are they cool or warm? (pause for a breath)

A shape appears before you through the purpley haze; the shape of a woman. She beckons you forward. As you walk towards her, she begins to dance. She invites you to join her. You gently start to sway as you feel in to your body, moving your feet, then your arms and your hips. You are in flow. As your body surrenders to the movement, your soul remembers the dance. Feel the moment. Dancing between the worlds.

As you dance you hear her call to you:

>*"Awaken...*
>*...Remember...*
>*...Untame...*
>*...Express...*
>*...Reclaim...*
>*...Embrace...*
>*...Unleash...*
>*...Release...*
>*...Unashamed...*
>*...Honour...*
>*...Exhale...*
>*...Exhale...*
>*...Exhale."*

You fall to the ground, and lie there, breathing deeply, thoroughly enchanted and exhilarated.

She comes to join you and you sit together on the ground.

How do you feel now?

As you get your breath back, she starts to speak:

"Thank you, Dear One. Thank you for joining me in your awakening and celebration of your true self. You are free and fully present in your power, uniting your body and soul together as one. You know who I am. I am you. You are me. We are She.
Now, is there anything you would like to ask me?"

(pause for as long as you need)

She stands and says:

"I must return to the mists, but know that I am always with you, and live deep within you. Whenever you need me I will help you. You are not alone."

She embraces you in a hug, but this is no ordinary hug. Her touch has untethered all your suppressed emotions and feelings that you have been keeping locked up and in check. (pause for a breath) As She relaxes her embrace, She has tears rolling down her cheeks:

"Feel all your feels and experience your emotions. This is all part of living your full and authentic life. This is your permission to do so. And this is my gift to you."

She presses something into your hands. You thank her and the mists begin to swirl once more. She fades back amongst the indigo, purple and lilac. And is gone.

You look down to your hands to see what She has placed there. What do you see? What has She gifted to you? (pause while you open your gift).

The mists have cleared and once again you are back in the wilds of before. All looks the same as it was prior to your dance with Her. But you are no longer the same woman who walked into the mists and walked back out.

How do you feel? (pause for a breath)

Take a soul deep breath in and begin to come back to the here and now. Take another deep breath in and wriggle your fingers and toes. On your next breath feel the floor beneath your feet and when you are ready, open your eyes.

Welcome back.

Journal Prompts

- Do I have a connection to the Divine Feminine? If so, what does She mean to me?
- Are there any deities I feel drawn to? Why?
- Do I connect with the Triple Aspect of the Goddess?
- What do I think of when I hear the words Spiritual and Spirituality?
- How do the words Spiritual and Spirituality make me feel?
- Do I look outside of myself for the answers rather than seeking from within? What am I seeking?
- Do I deem external knowledge, particularly printed or internet wisdom as more important than my own - especially when in conflict with my own experience or opinion? If so, why?
- Do I believe in magic?

- Are my beliefs something I've been told or something I've been drawn or called to?
- Did I connect with something because I read about it, was told about it or was informed that *this is the right way*?
- How often do I go outside? How often I do venture out to touch the earth, experience the seasons, connect with nature?
- What feelings do the words Witch and Priestess evoke in me?
- When I think of the word "connected" in terms of spirituality, to what is the connection with? Am I seeking that connection or am I already connected?
- Do I know who my ancestors were? If so, how far back and from where do they hail?
- Do I know my Red Thread, who my female ancestors were?
- Do I connect with the genus loci where I live? If so, how? If not, how can I?
- Are ethics and origins important to me in my practice? Do I or have I researched the history or backgrounds to my practices? If not why not?

Action

- Go outside, be barefoot and touch the earth, taste fresh produce, dance in the rain, talk to the wind, smell the flowers and hug a tree, moon bathe, swim in wild water, run free along the beach at the waters edge, or through the woods, open hillside or city parkland, star gaze or howl into the night.
- Observe the natural world in your local area, taking regular walks throughout the seasons and witness

the changes. What grows, and where, what can be foraged and used? Who lives there, ie birds or small mammals or insects.
- Notice how you feel in certain places, the energy of the place and within yourself.
- Explore what beliefs you have been brought up with regarding religion, if any, and see if they still hold true for you today.
- Create an altar space, it doesn't need to be a grand display, a spot on the window sill with a candle is ample, to sit by and gather your thoughts, just pause to breathe, to connect with yourself or with your ancestors or deity.
- Change your altar with the seasons, ie with fresh flowers or seasonal décor.
- Explore the different deities associated with where you live or where you are from, do you feel a connection to any?
- Review your current set up or practice and assess why you do what you do and if you need to or do so because you believe you have to?
- Consider what tools you currently use in your practice. Are they necessary or for fun?

THREAD FOUR

CIRCLES

From my hearth to yours.
From my heart to yours.
I see you, I hear you,
I honour you.
Fàilte .

Welcome to Circle, ladies ...

14

When We Gathered

The village raises the child.
The Circle honours the woman
~ Lissa Corra ~

Women gathering in Circle is a tradition as old as time, but a tradition destroyed over the many years by the Patriarchy, who succeeded in their mission to turn women against each other in competition rather than supporting each other as previous generations had done, where daughters learned from their mothers, aunts, older sisters, friends and grandmothers. Wisdom was passed down though generations, about what it was to be a woman; menstruation, birth, raising children, being a wife and/or a warrior, a teacher, a healer, a leader, a cook, a spinner, a weaver, a hunter, etc, as well as, of course, a sovereign being. Skills were shared, learned, taught and honed. Duties and responsibilities were similarly shared, e.g. child-rearing. This was the village. Women were respected, the elder women revered. They had knowledge, abilities and each other; they held the community together. There is an old Native American saying that states :

To destroy a village, destroy the Moon Lodge.

The Moon Lodge was the women's sacred Circle, their menstrual lodge, where they gathered. Not a menstrual hut where the women are cast out of the community whilst they bleed, as per what happens in some countries today such as in Nepal and their barbaric, and at times, fatal, practice of Chaupadi, but honoured as a special and sacred time. Time to rest, eat well and restore themselves for the following month ahead. During a women's bleeding time, it was believed that she was closer to the Divine and therefore she was powerful and wise.

When I initially heard about "Women's Circles" the first image that popped into my head was one of elderly ladies knitting and gossiping, or making jam in a *Women's Institute (WI)* type scenario. My only frame of reference for the *WI* was from the film *Calendar Girls* with Helen Mirren and Julie Walters. However, this was not to be the case.

The first Circle I ever attended wasn't a Moon Tent or Lodge, or preparing for a charity coffee morning. Instead I spent a Saturday afternoon in the company of a group of women, in the living room of a friend who hosted and arranged the Circle. The theme for the afternoon was 'Caring for Ourselves' and how exactly we do that. I was excited. My friend's home was cozy and I felt relaxed as we took up our space on the couch or chair or rug on the floor. We each brought some food for sharing, if memory serves me correctly, I brought cake (*Mr Kipling's French Fancies*, because who doesn't love a *French Fancy*?) whilst others brought home-made offerings. It was all welcome and was placed on the table where we helped ourselves to the communal feast as we pleased. We were ready to get into the purpose of the Circle and to discuss how we were looking after ourselves, or more importantly, how we were not.

I knew three of the women already and met the three others for the first time. It was comforting and re-assuring to hear similarities and inspiring to hear how other people do things, things that I thought, yes, I can do that too. The ages and life stages of the the women present weren't the same as mine - we had 3 generations of women there - Maidens, Mothers and Grandmothers. Our Circle was also shared with a beautiful five week old baby. To hear the different perspectives and stories passed between us all was fascinating. It was honest and refreshing.

I realised after the Circle was finished that the purpose wasn't, as I originally thought, the chosen topic of the Circle, but in fact the reality of gathering the women together, the sharing of stories and experiences in a safe space. The Circle itself.

A Circle was something I had wished to be part of again, but for the following couple of years I never found the time or place until I came across one on *Instagram*, to be held in Glasgow. The facilitator of the Circle and I had followed one another on *Instagram* and had mutual friends in common, but had never met in person or spoken to each other. When I saw her Circle appear on my feed I felt compelled to find out more.

I went along to the Circle, feeling a little apprehensive as I didn't know anyone else who was going. However, when I arrived at her front door, I was greeted with the most welcoming and warm hug and immediately felt so at home as I found my space in the Circle with the women who had arrived before me.

Our Circle held seven mothers, each with different stories yet each with an element of our own truth that resonated with every woman present. Through story and mediation, tea and relaxation, we shared that two hours in communal nourishment of the soul. I filled my cup back up, without the usual "mother's guilt" that goes hand in hand with time out for myself. And I didn't want to leave.

This is such an ancient tradition that had been lost but has since been rediscovered and for that I am thankful. To be part of, and, sit in Circle like this was just the medicine I needed, so I wrote myself a prescription to attend the next one.

In 2017 I began holding Circles of my own. They took place in my living room and in the woods until I found a studio that allowed for regular Circles in a dedicated space.

To honour my 40th birthday I gathered my sisters in sacred Circle and celebrated a beautiful and emotional time. Nine of us sat in my living room and each played a part in the ceremony, telling stories, guiding the rest of us in meditation, crafting, poetry, song and ritual. I felt incredibly blessed as my friend led the ceremony of leaving my thirties, with it's lessons, regrets, achievements and acknowledgements, moving forward to face and embrace any fears of growing older (I have none, I LOVE this ageing process with the wisdom it brings) and set intentions for this coming stage of my life. These women in my clan of choice also set intentions and wishes for me, which were burnt to release said intentions in the central cauldron. My good old broom was put to good use in symbolically clearing away the old to make space for the new and with a twist on the the matrimonial jumping of the broom, I jumped my broom to cross over into this new phase and exciting times ahead. Not a typical 40th birthday celebration, but a deeply felt one.

The old adage of it taking a village to raise a child is something I had no experience of, yet yearned for, in the early years of my parenting journey. I am truly thankful and grateful that that village has since been created and blossomed into the wonderful community and friendships that it has, and is one which I whole heartedly trust, respect and cherish. But it is not just children that need raising. We, as adults, also need the strength and support and the safe space to be seen, heard and held, in order to continue to rise. The support that can only be found amongst a select sacred few; those precious women with whom you gather. The Circle. The women of the family, friendship group, the village and Circle may or may not be the same women, that's not the point. The point is, we don't have to do this alone, any of it, in this thing we call life. Those of us with partners will also find that the power of true sisterhood from Circle is immeasurable.

Lessons learned in the old village included self respect, trusting their own intuition as to what feels right or doesn't in any given situation, and discovering the workings of life without any fear of shame or embarrassment. Learning not just the biological function of the menstrual cycle but how to live with it and how to best understand what each of the phases of each month meant - again intuition around listening to and knowing their own body.

Being in Circle, gaining the wisdom and learning the teachings, allowed for the self confidence to be able stand up in and for truth, to enable body autonomy, the ability to determine personal boundaries and authority to honour them, meaning that they did not tolerate or put up with shit and dealt with any at that time, not years later. (#metoo immediately springs to mind here).

The time to bring back the Sacred Circles and initiate our daughters, nieces, friend's daughters, mothers and grannies into the fold, into their power, in the safety of those who love and trust, is now.

15

Why We Gather

Women gathering together in Circle is support, is self-care, is healing, is vital.
~ Lissa Corra ~

When women gather together in Circle there is an unspoken bond, a sense of community, familiarity and sisterhood. Even amongst strangers. How do I know? I know because have I experienced these very sensations and feelings, each and every time I have sat in Circle.

***Bringing back the village,
one Circle at a time.***

When women gather together to talk freely and be witnessed without judgement, it is a beautiful thing and it is where the healing takes place. We learn from each other and unlearn the conditioned programming. All we need is community, support and an understanding that we are not each other's competition.

That all sounds wonderful, but what actually *is* a Women's Circle? A Women's Circle or Sacred Sister Circle (or any other name given to it) is a dedicated space for women to come together, usually for a couple of hours, to share in each other's lives with their stories, truths, real feelings, to be heard and supported. It is a place to learn, to release, to grow, to know (yourself) and just take some time out for you, to reflect, be inspired and develop friendships. It's a place and space to just *be;* to be honest and free, let your guard down, for fellow sisters in Circle to hold the space for you and for each other. It's not gossip or judgement, it's not material surface "stuff". Instead it is where we allow the healing power of speaking your truth while releasing the tears without the need to be coddled or comforted and be told that everything will be okay. This is a powerful place. A Women's Circle provides a chance to connect with a deep understanding, appreciation and trust of and in ourselves and each other.

You might wonder whether you need to go to a Circle or what the point of going would be when you have already found your "tribe", so to speak. You already have close knit group of friends who offer support, solidarity, advice, fun and friendship spanning years, perhaps decades, of shared experiences. Great, that's wonderful to cherish and hold onto, but it may also be something that many people don't actually have, or at least not on that level. I ask you to consider how else a regular Circle may enrich your life? A Circle is different from having a "girl's night" with your pals.

There is a reason that Circles are having their moment now. There is a soul deep longing for the village, for cross generational wisdom and teachings and relearning; for connection with community and like minds and enquiring minds, for confidence in rising up and reclaiming our place in society out from the shadows of the Patriarchy, and for being authentic and true to who we are or want to be rather than who are supposed to be. For some people that is scary and they need the sisterhood.

The Circles I hold centre around reconnecting to our community, re-establishing the village. There is always a guided meditation, ritual, song, journalling and sharing in discussion on a chosen theme for that particular Circle. Each woman experiences the joy of being heard, seen and emotionally, spiritually or physically held, whilst offering the same experience to the women in the Circle.

Pre-pandemic, I loved my Circles on a Saturday morning and Thursday evening, a gentle yet empowering start to the weekend or shaking off of the last vestiges of the day in a relaxing environment. Space to breathe and cast off the cloak and mask of who we are on the outside to acknowledge and embrace who we are on the inside. We are a village, we are a community and the sisterhood bond is wound around what we want and need not on what patriarchal society has decreed.

> **The joys, the tears, the laughter, the love the truths, the challenges, all held within the circle. There lies its power and strength.**

A regular Circle becomes an anchor in life, a deliberate, conscious choice to take the time to press that pause button, reconnect with your needs, release any emotions or thoughts that are not serving you and just relax, replenishing your soul with love, tea and ritual. It is a beautiful experience, but it is not all love and light, it is a real and raw experience and tears often flow. Those tears are so healing; an exhale. Sometime we release, sometime we hold the space to allow another to release.

The power and strength of a regular Circle is so restorative and I'd say, vital, to our health and well being. The power of Circle is in its structure; its completeness and wholeness, the masculine container to allow the feminine flow of creation, manifestation and emotion, it's the womb, the pelvic bowl, it is Earth and grounding, stable and strong. What a combination! It is the vessel that holds all the juices of life that each person within that Circle brings. There is no shame when stories are shared within the sanctuary of a Women's Circle. You are free from patriarchal conditioning and free to be yourself.

When women gather in circle, ripples are created, healing takes place. For all of us.

I have mentioned previously in the book about bringing the younger girls and women into the Circle and share the wisdoms with them but the Circle community doesn't just support the Maiden, it supports her Mother too. Having the support to guide her daughter through these turbulent years, knowing that she is not doing it all alone, even when there is conflict of opinion as the daughter is establishing her individuality and differentiating herself from her mother, she is not alone. There is also the additional comfort in knowing that if the Mother can't assist her daughter for whatever reason, there is another woman/women there who can. This is not to drive wedges between the mother/daughter relationship but to strengthen the bond and give each enough space to breath and grow. That very same mother may be the support a different maiden turns to when in need. The web of the Circle is being continually woven.

When I think back to all the #metoo situations I have experienced, I am frustrated with myself for not speaking up as well as being angry with the situations, but am convinced that while those situations wouldn't necessarily *not* have happened, they would have instead been called out at the time and dealt with appropriately and I would have been supported too.

We also need to welcome the Crones, the elders, our older women into the Circle. This may be a completely alien concept to them and topics such as the menopause and ageing and value or self worth may be considered something to deal with privately by yourself. There is much to learn from our elders and much they can perhaps unlearn too, for themselves from the younger women. When we welcome our women and recreate our village, the lessons are learned, both forwards and backwards, through the threads of time, connecting to our ancestors and descendants, healing all along the line. The connection and support flows all through the ages and benefits the collective.

Circles are the Anti-Bitch.

I have been told that Circles can't work as women are too bitchy, catty, competitive, judgemental, name another label that keeps pitting women against women. THIS in itself is a reason FOR Circles. Circles are the Anti-Bitch. They foster belonging, connection and friendships founded in a shared bond, respect, understanding. We bear witness to each others soul and truth. Circles are raw but safe. We each see or feel something of ourselves in every other woman in the Circle. Some women I have circled with know me better than friends I have had for years, through sharing of our truths and real experience, no masks. Not everyone has to like everyone else, as is the way in life, but there remains a connection, a belonging to the Circle and its members. You know that no matter what, you are always welcome. If it's your first ever Circle and you arrive knowing no-one, you certainly won't leave that way. In fact if ever there was a theme song for Circles it has to be the one from the 70s and 80s telly programme *Cheers* (I used to LOVE *Cheers*!) Join in if you know it, and join in if you don't!

> ***Making your way in the world today***
> ***takes everything you've got.***
> ***Taking a break from all your worries,***
> ***sure would help a lot.***
> ***Wouldn't you like to get away?***
> ***Sometimes you want to go***
> ***where everybody knows your name,***
> ***and they're always glad you came.***
> ***You wanna be where you can see,***
> ***our troubles are all the same.***
> ***You wanna be where everybody knows***
> ***your name.***
> ~ *Gary Portnoy & Judy Hart Angelo* ~

Here, I just got fair emotional singing away to that, proper choked up. I am clearly in need of a Circle!

We are a social species, and while I, as an introvert, have enjoyed and benefited from some aspects of the lock down restrictions, I miss gathering with other women in Circle; I miss the discussions, the physical connection, the community of mutual support. When we gather, particularly post lock down, the healing will truly begin.

Up until fairly recently, talking about our emotions and feelings was considered improper, a sign of weakness and bad manners. Keep your troubles at home, maintain the British stiff upper lip, hold your water and keeping your own counsel were how we dealt with things. Everything came down to appearances. Naturally therefore, opening up and sharing your real emotions and thoughts and fears and accomplishments and joy while sat in a Circle may seem like an uncomfortable stretch eliciting an *"oh hell, no"* reaction at the mere thought. Trust me, it'll be the most beneficial thing you do to free yourself from the constraints of social constructs and expectations. Sharing in this manner is our strength. It is supported by being heard for its truth and without any associated drama. In circle you reclaim and honour your dignity with the telling of your story. And my goodness, you will also laugh. A LOT!

Gathering in circle is an act of self care, self love and much needed today, yesterday and tomorrow. The power of Circle. For all of us.

Awaken Your Wild You

16

How We Gather

What is shared in Circle stays in Circle.

In Circle, the golden rule is "*what's shared in Circle stays in Circle*". Without that trust we cannot begin to heal, be authentic and true; have the freedom and space to be witnessed for who we really are, to explore the depths of our soul and unpick the societal learnings we have been taught.

To Circle is to gather in a space and time out of time, to take a much needed break from the everyday, to reconnect with ourselves, to pause, breathe, relax and nourish our being. The Circle is a safe and sacred container, fully supporting each woman present as she needs. This is such an ancient tradition that has been lost, rediscovered and revived.

Circles are enjoying a resurgence and are currently back in vogue, where I hope they will remain. There are so many different types of Circles popping up and taking place regularly, both online and in-person. I have been to and held many different types of Circles over the years, including various general Women's Circles where the women present spanned the generations of Maiden/Mother/Crone and the discussions were richer because of it; Mother's Circles where it was incredibly healing to know that we, as mothers, while we may have different styles of parenting, all share so many similar experiences and emotions. It was a real tonic for those mothering wobbles we rarely admit to with others; Full Moon and New Moon Circles where we were letting go of what no longer served us and setting new intentions. These were incredibly cathartic and whilst we met with our shadow (hidden) selves they were such joyful experiences; Drumming Circles, are a new style of Circle for me, held by a friend which was such a powerful and emotional one as it brought up so many feelings with the primal drum beat; I have also participated in mixing Circling with ecstatic dance which was another incredible form of expression and release.

Other types of circles taking place are Mother~Daughter Circles, Sacred Sister Circles, Goddess Circles, Monthly Circles, Weekly Circles, Red Tent and Moon Lodge Circles, Covens even, plus a wheen more. I have sat in Circle on the floors of living rooms in women's homes, cabins in their gardens, in the depths of the woods around a fire (a firm favourite), in dance studios, yoga studios, complementary health stores, and on Zoom. Each providing a different yet equally comforting space.

You may think you have never been to a Circle before, but have you ever been to a baby shower, sharing your own birth experience or parenting tips with the Mother-to-be or storing away useful nuggets of insights for the future? A hen night, sharing and celebrating stories of marriage with its ups and downs, passing on advice and experience? Sat around a campfire chatting and telling stories? A

Tupperware or *Body Shop* or candle party, showing up to support your pal and buying stuff you don't need or particularly want so she can earn her free gift? A group meeting where the general discussion happens in the round? These too, are Circles of a sort. Granted, not a gathering whose purpose is for going soul deep, but a deliberate and supportive, generally celebratory coming together nonetheless.

So what is involved in an actual Circle then? How do we Circle? Come with me through my set up and ritual of facilitating a Sacred Women's Circle:

Set up

The Circle is centred around the altar space which I create for each Circle. The altar is important as it is the focal point around which we all sit and into which we each contribute. It is important to me that the altar looks beautiful as well as serving a practical function. Everything that is held in the altar space is there for a reason.

So, starting in the centre I have my cauldron in which is placed a pillar candle. I prefer a white candle but any colour will work, perhaps incorporating a colour specific to the season such as orange for autumn of green for spring for instance. The cauldron holds the light, it symbolises transformation, the womb, the divine, the magic. It also serves us in ritual later on in the Circle. Around the base of the cauldron I have a circle of dried rowan berries (for protection) and sometimes a ring of horse chestnuts (aka conkers or cheggies. Did you know you can make soap from them? That's another story for another book.) for clarity and cleansing. Then I place a ring of tea lights, one for each sister attending. Underneath the cauldron sometimes I place crystals if the mood takes me and I feel they are appropriate or significant. From there I acknowledge the four directions, East, South, West and North and place items there to represent each; a feather for air in the east, incense for fire in the south, chalice of water for water in the west and crystals for earth in the north, sometime I will place art work or statues in the directional quadrants too, each representing the four phases of woman, maiden, mother, wild woman, crone. The Circle altar always looks beautiful with fresh flowers placed around it. Using fresh, seasonal fruit, berries and plant cuttings adds to the beauty of the space and the connection to the season. I have two pomegranate dishes placed in the circle holding affirmations for the sisters to select and journal prompts too. After that, I may spread a circle of tarot or oracle cards (or both). And that completes the altar at this stage.

Outside of and around the altar I set out cushions for the women to sit on, each with a flower to take home and a pen and paper for use during the Circle. The space is set, leaving just the tea and cake to arrange and music to play. I have a separate soundtrack for each Circle I have held, music picked specifically for that occasion.

Welcome

Upon arrival, the women are welcomed into the space with a hug and cuppa, the music is playing in the background (*I Am Woman* by Helen Reddie is ALWAYS on the play list), and there is time for a quick hello and blether amongst the women before I call them in.

We gather round the altar space and get comfy sat on the cushions. I open the circle with a small blessing (from the start of this thread):

> *From my hearth to yours.*
> *From my heart to yours.*
> *I see you, I hear you,*
> *I honour you.*
> *Fàilte .*
> *Welcome to Circle, ladies ...*

and I light the candle in the cauldron. If there are any new women present for the first time, I go over Circle Etiquette, such as the all important, "what's shared in Circle stays in Circle", as well as the understanding that there is no pressure to speak if she doesn't want to, she can instead just listen, witness and support. There is **no** offering of unsolicited advice and **no** interrupting when someone is sharing. We use a speaking piece which happens to be my matryoshka doll, which is passed around the Circle.

Holding the speaking piece means that woman has the space and time to speak and share without interruption. When she is finished she passes it on to the next person who wishes to speak, not necessarily the person sitting beside her. Unless a woman specifically asks for advice or feedback, none is given, she is purely heard and witnessed.

The conversations that need to be aired are meant to be shared at this time, trusting the moment.

If no new sisters, then we head straight into the introductions. Each person in turn introduces themselves (there is power in declaring your name aloud, and also your lineage if you know it), share why they are here in this Circle and add a little token of themselves to the altar. Items such as pieces of jewellery, photos, sacred and much loved trinkets, crystals, oracle cards, sentimental items, even a fridge magnet (mine) have all been added over the time I have been holding Circles. The women take them back home at the end, I don't collect them as treasure! Before moving onto the next person, she will take an affirmation (and if it resonates, she is welcome to read it aloud and share her thought on it) and a journal prompt. Lastly she lights her tea light from the cauldron candle and sets it down in the centre of the altar, confirming her place in the Circle.

Body of the Circle

There is always a guided meditation and the main section of the Circle is then open for discussion on the theme I have chosen. We have a tea break and during this time some women will pull an oracle or tarot card and there is general chat or time taken to write down anything important that has come up during the first half of the Circle.

After the break we continue the discussion. One of the fascinating things about the open share is that you never know where the conversation is going to go or what someone will bring up that others connect with or gives us cause to pause or ponder.

The most looked-forward-to parts of my Circles is the ritual. Once the discussion has been brought to a close, it is time to get the pen and paper out. We take a few minutes to ourselves to think about what has passed between us, reflect up on our feelings and potential actions going forwards. We write down on the paper either something that we wish to draw in or release and let go of, it could be an emotion, a habit, an association with how we feel about ourselves or a situation, anything pertaining to the the Circle's theme and we take turns by declaring our intention and then burning it in the flames of the cauldron. The joy this small action brings, delights me every time, especially when new Circle attendees have their turn. Burning is not always possible so adding salt to water and stating the intention aloud as sprinkling the salt is an alternative (then pouring the water out on to the earth afterwards, or at the appropriate lunar phase).

Closing the Circle

Bringing the Circle to a close is very much a ritual itself. We stand and sing a song that I love which closes the Circle perfectly. I used to just play it from Spotify, but the sound of us all singing together is goose bump inducing and so powerful. Pre-covid, I then passed around a cup of friendship, quaiche style. Each took a sip of my warmed home-made non-alcoholic cider, expressed their thanks to one another for our time together and passed the cup round back to me. Just as I open the Circle with a blessing, I close it in the same fashion:

> ***From my hearth to yours.***
> ***From my heart to yours.***
> ***I thank you***
> ***with deepest gratitude***
> ***for all you have brought,***
> ***shared, and all you will***
> ***take with you onwards.***
> ***Beannachd***

and extinguish the cauldron flame.

Over the years I have facilitated different types of circles. My women's Circles have a pre-set theme that is the focus of our shared time in that particular Circle, such as a phase of woman's life cycle, a seasons of the year, a phase of the lunar cycle, on the topic of self care or healing the sister wound. Each Circle opens up so many stories and experiences, points of view and opportunities for growth. The Festive Circle I held at Christmas one year had one of the women teaching us belly dancing. She had choreographed a routine for us to a Christmas song, it was incredible! My 40th Circle was an especially powerful Circle, so too was the one I held, in memory of a loved friend who had died. The remembrance Circle allowed each of us the opportunity to say goodbye to our friend and to have our moment to say the things we never got the chance to when she was still earthside. It was enormously healing and offered a safe place to express our grief and share in celebration of the life our friend lived.

Just as lock down hit I had to press pause on in-person ceremonies, including the menarche Circle for a young lady of 12 years who was to celebrate her rite of passage witnessed by her mum, her gran and a small group of trusted friends, welcoming her into the cycling years with their dedication to help her navigate them, supported. It is a beautiful ceremony and very special time to honour.

If you feel excited to Circle with women, either your mates or looking for like minded women but not sure where to find them, either set up your own Circle or find one in your town or city, I guarantee there will be Circles happening in local community centres or more probably in people's living rooms (where most the Circles I have attended have taken place). If you don't have a village or circle of your chosen family, know that they are out there and will hear your call. I know because it was what I needed and what I found. The power of Circle is found in creating your village, community and sisterhood, in the honouring and reclaiming of our rites of passage, and in the sharing of skills, knowledge and traditions within the Circle. It is medicine.

17

Remember Reconnect Reclaim

Meditation

In a circle of women

Sitting or lying comfortably, close your eyes. Imagine a light around your entire body, softly glowing, blurring the edges of you. Notice what colour it is. Take a deep breath in though your nose, and as you exhale the light glows a little brighter. Take another deep breath in, this time filling up your heart centre. On the exhale notice if the light glows even brighter or if it changes colour. On you next breath, inhale all the way down to your womb space, and on the exhale the colour enveloping your body becomes bright and bold. What colour is it now?

Pause for a deep breath, and as you breathe you notice that you are standing at a threshold. The entrance into which is red. Is it a door or a curtain or a red glow emanating from within? You are curious and cross the threshold. You find your self in a circular room. It is warm and the fragrance is very pleasing to your nose. The room is lit with candles around the room on wall sconces and a beautiful candelabra from the ceiling. You can hear the rhythm of drum beat and feel it resonate within your body.

There are 4 women in discussion at the far side of the room. They turn to look at you when you enter, with smiles upon their faces. They walk over towards you and each in turn embraces you in a warm, welcoming hug. The eldest of the women says :

"Welcome, we've been waiting for you"

She looks familiar to you but you are not sure from where. Take a moment to look at her; how tall is she, what colour is her hair, what is she wearing, how old is she? (pause to look at her) The woman to her left is younger, middle aged. She also has a familiarity about her. What do you observe about her? (pause again) The woman on the elder woman's right is younger again and also known to you from a time in your mind. She is fuller in figure. What else do you notice about her appearance? (pause) The woman to your left is the youngest. You already know that you know her, but from where? What does she look like? What is she wearing? (pause)

The elder woman speaks:

"Come join us in Circle, there is a space waiting for you."

She leads you and the other three women into the middle of the room where cushions of all sizes and shades of red, orange, pink and purple are arranged. Warm blankets are scattered around too. The Circle looks so inviting. You take your position in the Circle, sinking into the soft cushions. In the middle of the Circle there is a beautiful arrangement of flowers and plants, fruits, berries, nuts and dark chocolate. There are more candles and figurines, large and small decorating this altar space. Every where you look you see something else to pique your interest. Pause for a moment to observe how you feel.

Four more women appear and join you in the Circle. They are friendly and smile warmly, greeting you by name. Two of them you know instantly. They are the dearest and closest women to you in your life. Nine of you are now seated around the Circle. The elder woman lights the large pillar candle on the central altar and opens the Circle with a blessing :

"From my hearth to yours.
From my heart to yours.
I see you, I hear you,
I honour you.
Fàilte .
Welcome to Circle, ladies.

She continues:

"We are gathered here in this Circle to welcome our Dear One into the mysteries and into the sacred sisterhood.

This Circle is here today in your honour, my Dear."

The woman to her right then introduces herself to you:

"Welcome Dear One. I am your inner Wild. I love you. Thank you for finding your way here on your awakening journey."

She takes a smaller candle and lights it from the central one. The woman on her right then speaks:

"Welcome Dear One. You know who I am. I love you. Thank you for finding your way here on your awakening journey."

She too takes a smaller candle and lights it from the central one. The women continue round, moonwise, introducing themselves in turn and lighting their candle:

"Welcome Dear One. I am here representing your ancestral lineage. We love you. Thank you for finding your way here on your awakening journey."

"Welcome Dear One. I am your inner Mother. I love you. Thank you for finding your way here on your awakening journey."

"Welcome Dear One. I am here representing your descendants. We love you. Thank you for finding your way here on your awakening journey."

"Welcome Dear One. I am your inner Maiden. Thank you for finding your way here on your awakening journey."

"Welcome Dear One. You know who I am. I love you.

Thank you for finding your way here on your awakening journey."

"Welcome Dear One. I am your inner Crone and Wise Woman. I love you. Thank you for finding your way here on your awakening journey."

The introductions reach you. You introduce yourself to the Circle (pause to introduce) and light your own candle, confirming your place in the Circle, with the collective.

The Wise Woman again speaks :

"Thank you each and everyone. My Dear One, you may ask us anything and share anything that needs to be released. You will be witnessed. Know that you are cherished and held in love; we are a reflection of you. We will share the mysteries of the bloods, our sacred rites and the wisdom of the Divine Feminine. We are here to heal, to honour and to hear you. When you are ready, the Circle is ready for you."

Take a slow breath. The time is yours, take as much as you need to experience your Circle. Connect with your women, your Circle. Embrace their wisdom and knowledge, their comfort and strength. (pause for 30 minutes)

The Wise Woman speaks :

"Thank you Dear One for surrendering to this beautiful Circle, our time here is sacred. I invite all of you to join hands and give your fellow sisters' hand a squeeze, a squeeze of solidarity, support and sisterhood. I close this Circle and offer my blessing to you all.

*From my hearth to yours.
From my heart to yours.
I thank you
with deepest gratitude
for all you have brought,
shared, and all you will
take with you onwards.
Beannachd"*

She extinguishes the central candle and closes the Circle. How do you feel now, how does your body feel? (pause)

You rise from the comfortable position in Circle and bid your sisters farewell, until the next time, for there will be a next time that you will gather together.

You exit through the threshold, back to the other side, back to the light enveloping your body. What colour is that aura surrounding you? Take a deep breath in and as you exhale, notice the glow start to subdue. Does it change colour or softy fade? On your next inhale, bring you awareness to your limbs and beginning to gently move them and feel into them. As you exhale, pay attention to the glow and its colour. As you inhale on this breath, breathe the remaining glow into your body, into your heart. And as you exhale, release every ounce of breath as you bring yourself back to the present. When you are ready, open your eyes.

Welcome back.

Journal Prompts

- What was my initial thought upon learning of Women's Circles?

- Would I like to go to one?
- What benefits would circling bring to my life?
- What obstacles might there be to attending a Circle?
- Are there any parts of Women's Circle that make me feel uncomfortable?
- If I don't think a Women's Circle is for me, why do I believe this to be so?
- Who would I like to Circle with?
- Who do I know that may benefit from a Women's Circle?
- Do I want to be part of this tradition and incorporate it into my life?
- Would a Circle have aided me in my younger years? How?
- Would a Circle aid my in my future? How?
- Could I host a Circle? Do I want to?

Action

- Search for Circles in your local area or online (Instagram and Facebook are great places to start).
- Attend one of the Circles.
- Pick a theme you would most like to discuss in a Circle environment.
- Gather your close friends, a group of 4 is ample to start with, and host a Circle in your garden or in your living room
- Set up a zoom meeting and host a virtual Circle with your friends or family members.
- Create a ritual for you and the other women in Circle to participate in during your gathering.
- Take it in turns with your Circle group to facilitate and host the Circle, that way everyone gets to relax

and enjoy the experience as well as hold the space and keep the time for the Circle.
- Create a playlist of music for your Circle, to listen to as background music, to play alongside a meditation or to sing along with as part of the Circle.

THREAD FIVE

SACRED

Pause, rest and just breathe.
And sleep too.
Eat well and drink plenty water.
Sleep some more, take time out to just be.
Simply say "NO".
Then figure out what's next.
In your own time.
Caw canny on the expectations!
Pause, rest, breathe,
And know that that is enough.
No over thinking, second guessing,
over analysing, justifying or apologising.
Just breathe.

~ Lissa Corra ~

18

Sacred Soul Sustenance

Making ourselves a priority not an afterthought is a necessity
~ Lissa Corra ~

Question: What does our lifestyle have to do with awakening our inner Wild and reclaiming our sovereignty? Answer: Everything!

How we go about our every day, how we schedule our week, how we prioritise our activities, tasks, chores, responsibilities, health, time and more; the combination of our habits and going through the motions of the mundane with the choices we deliberately make, creates the life we live. When was the last time you thought about the life you lead, how you live it and whether it is one you love, one that is sacred, fulfilling and sovereign?

Four years ago I had a passion, a path and a practice that I had been journeying with for years, parts of it for some 20+ years, but it was a secret. Fear of ridicule kept it hidden and kept my voice small regarding the matters that ignite my fire. (Who knew there was more to me than my opinions and politics?) Staying small and insignificant when I had so much to share was frustrating but it was safe. Thankfully times are changing and have changed enough for me to share my passions and knowledge, and to bring my blog and resulting business into creation and now the courage to write this book. My husband is my biggest supporter, championing my crazy and proudly waving my freak flag alongside me. While he may not fully understand the whys and whats of my practice, he understands that I need to be able to create and express myself and that at times I need space and solitude. I am grateful to have a partner that "gets" me and respects that side of me. That understanding allows for me to be able to manage the other areas of life in a more sane fashion.

To write your best story, awaken your Wild and reclaim your sovereignty may, and probably will, require some changes in your lifestyle, which can seem like an intimidating prospect. It requires honesty and vulnerability, inner strength and determination. Not everyone will understand, but then, they're not meant to. This is your life and YOU understand it. We are all on our own journey, each path as unique as each person. Your chosen route may be a head scratcher for some (mine certainly is), but that's okay because it's yours not theirs; would you want to switch? You've got your path and are on your journey, not necessarily with a map, the destination may be unknown, but it is sacred. And it is yours to wander.

It is my belief and experience that in order to make the changes and create the life we want, need and deserve, we must begin with looking after ourselves properly; honouring, nourishing and loving ourselves as we would our most loved one(s). I am reluctant to use the expression, "self care" here as it is so clichéd. Yes it describes perfectly what I am about to share with you but it does lend itself all too well to an eye-roll, so I am going to rephrase it as Sacred Soul Sustenance (and I do adore alliteration even if it does sound a little pretentious, okay, a big bit pretentious. I just find "Self Care" to be so blah and beige).

Sacred Soul Sustenance will, like almost everything else in this book, look and be experienced differently by every single individual. What I am going to share here are some suggestions of types of things we can do to ensure we are sustaining our life force and identifying potential barriers that prevent us from doing so.

Firstly, can we just agree that SSS is compulsory and non-negotiable? Not in a dictatorial sense, just an acknowledgement that if you don't prioritise it no-one else will. It is not self-*ish* but is self respect, self preservation and a huge part of self love. It is vital for our own health and well-being as well as for that of those who depend upon us too. Remember the in-flight instructions to ensure you put on your own oxygen mask before helping anyone else? (The other cliché in the self care realm, but with good reason) This nugget of advice applies to many areas of our lives, not just when we are heading off on holiday.

Okay, so here we go. Let us look at the different ways we can ensure we make the effort, and if need be, create the time and space for that all important Sacred Soul Sustenance, starting with getting enough rest. It is essential to ensure we sufficiently rest and recharge.

Restore. Revitalise. Relax. Recover.
Replenish. Renew. Revive. Refresh.
It doesn't matter what you call it,
just make sure you refilleth thy cup!

Please remember that as women, we are cyclic creatures, just like nature herself. We are not built to keep going like the popular bunny in the battery adverts, in a constant linear fashion, or just like the bunny, we will eventually run out of juice. Burnout is not something to aspire to. Having been there and done that, I can attest that it has no place on your bucket list. Neither too has the stress, frustration and resulting resentment riding shotgun on the journey. Instead, we respect the ebbs and flows of our cycle through the month, and we pause, and just exhale as we need, be it daily, weekly or monthly, or when YOU decide.

When I hear the buzz word self-care, I automatically think bubble bath, candles, wine or gin. However, that is not what I mean here. When you hear Sacred Soul Sustenance I want you to think about looking after you, all of you; mind body and spirit. Not bubble baths but instead integrity and accountability. These are fundamental components to supporting yourself, bypassing them for a candle lit bubble bath is not caring for the whole of you or doing you any favours in the now or the future. Own your own shit, it's part of who you are/were and gives you a choice to see and to know if it is who you will be. No-one said this would be pretty but it's real. Enjoy a bubble bath by all means, I love a soak with a good book and a glass of wine or mug of tea, but it isn't the be all and end all of looking after oneself. Being honest, sovereign and in alignment with your truth and actions will stand you in better stead.

Do you ever have that gnawing feeling eating away at you with a never ending list of "shoulds" that need tending to before you are allowed to do something for yourself? You are hastily added to the bottom of said list, as an after thought, as another should, but the one that is perpetually just out of reach. If by some miracle you achieve the holy grail of "me time", you are greeted by good old guilt. How dare you be so lazy or self indulgent. Making the shift to incorporating even the tiniest of changes to prioritising yourself is imperative. Baby steps are good, they are a start and move you in the right direction.

So, back to actively achieving the mission of getting our required rest. Here are my 6 top tips to getting a good rest :

- Sleep. No shit Sherlock! But seriously - how many of us get the recommended 7-8 hours per night? Nope, I thought not. Are you squeezing some "me time" in after the kids go to bed, and/or getting up super early before the rest of the household to grab an hour before the to-do list kicks in? (the latter being my preference.) A few years ago I read *Thrive: The Third Metric to Redefining Success and Creating a Happier Life* by Arianna Huffington, where she recommended scheduling bed time. Actually putting bedtime in your planner or on your calendar alongside dental appointments, work commitments, kids sports activities etc. It made perfect sense. We wouldn't be late for any of our other appointments, and our sleep is definitely one which we don't want to miss. As practical an idea as it is, it is still a work of discipline to ensure the time is met.
- Take a nap. Toddlers are proof that a nap is necessary to refresh and revive oneself. While we are obviously not toddlers, a quick 20 minute power nap has been proven, by science, and Claudia Winkleman in her book, *Quite*, to be incredibly beneficial to our well being, creativity and productivity.
- Ditch the alarm clock, even just once a week (if you have kids and a partner, let your significant other get on with the breakfast routine and morning shenanigans) and rise with the sun. This sounds more appealing in the darker winter months, but what I am driving at, is to say, let your body wake up

- naturally when it is ready, and therefore had enough rest.
- If using your alarm, don't snooze it. This may seem counter intuitive, as the more snoozes means the more rest, right? Nope, it's a fallacy. The more you snooze, the more unrested you become, cue that groggy discombobulated feeling we get. The constant re-waking of the brain confuses it and makes us feel worse.
- No phones in bed! Since I stopped using my phone as an alarm clock (got a proper clock instead) there is no need for my phone to be beside my bed, which means no late night scrolling, no keeping my brain alert and switched on and therefore inhibiting sleep. I fall asleep quicker and more soundly. Less screens generally is a good thing but it is important to switch them off an hour before going to sleep inorder to let your brain unwind.
- Admitting defeat in accepting the rest. Sometimes we can't focus and stay in the zone, sometime our heads are being turned in another direction. Sometimes we have to give in to the distraction and recognise it as a form of rest; admitting defeat is accepting the rest. They do say a change is as good as a rest, for a reason!

To accept a day that is not particularly productive is to know that perhaps you just needed the time and head space to allow the new ideas of tomorrow to form.

Okay, so we have established that sufficient rest is sacrosanct. Now what? Simplicity, that's what.

Simplicity can have such profound effects on absolutely any part of your life from your home, your relationships, your routines, your meals, your finances, your digital world, your inner thoughts, your wardrobe, your personal spiritual practice and more. I'm not talking here about *KonMari*-ing your entire home, but if that's your jam, go hug your belongings and see if they spark joy – I did three or four years ago and is was amazing (the decluttering I mean, not the joy-seeking hugging of inanimate objects). Uncluttered simplicity was something this clutterbug-boho-maximalist had aspired to and longed for, for years. I adore minimalist images on line, they look so peaceful and calm and gentle. I also had a yearning for a content and simple life without drama, distraction and chaos. (We can all dream, right?)

For my fellow Gen X-ers, do you remember what life was like back in the early - mid 90s when mobile phones weren't thing? What a unknown luxury that freedom was. Perhaps an unrealistic end goal of mine to want to reclaim that level of analogue in the digital times we live in today, but it was a real desire none the less. And that is the simplicity I want to talk about.

Life has gotten all rather intense in modern times, what with the constant feed of information from our computers, tablets, phones, 24hour TV channels and radio. We have social media where we are forever plugged into what is happening at any given time around the world to friends and family, long-lost friends, 'friends' we haven seen or spoken to since school, and to strangers. We are being told how live our lives from every aspect. There are labels for everything and everyone - we have to conform to and fit in to *something*. The political world is playing a massive game of Kerplunk, morals and ethics are in free fall. Pick a side. And that is without even mentioning the global pandemic that has been doing the rounds in waves; CovidFest World

Tour 2020 ain't done yet, here comes its third encore for the masses.

Have you tried to simplify your intake from the infinite avalanche of information? We all know that taking a Social Media holiday is good for us, especially if we use numerous platforms on a regular basis. But do we need to take a break from the screens or the content of our screens? Are we addicted to *Facebook* or just our phones? These are questions I have pondered many times over the past decade, since I got my first smart phone at the start of 2012. The same question that popped into my head when I was feeling frustrated and anxious and numb and bored and happy and joyful and tired all at the same time, every time I picked up my phone and began the habitual scrolling.

I have taken social media breaks and detoxes many times, a week here a month there as well as reducing screen time generally, including binge watching *Netflix* or auto play on *YouTube*. The sole purpose being to slooooooooow down and appreciate real life on the daily, following my instincts rather than algorithms. And every time I've done this, I have learned new lessons and re-affirmed what I already knew BUT I always, always, always fell straight back into the old habits. My notifications had all been turned off since I don't remember when, my phone was always on silent, it didn't even vibrate, yet still I had the compulsion to "check" it. I even uninstalled the social media apps, having instead to go through my browser to partake in the aforementioned "checking". It had become mentally exhausting and somewhat toxic when dealing with some people. The time lost to that scrolling is just that; lost. Forever! What a complete waste of time and energy. And for what, really, at the end of the day? I genuinely believe I have an actual addiction to my smart phone and social media. When I got my *iphone* in 2019 I started checking how often I was using it and the number of pickups. I was disgusted, properly ashamed and horrified by just how much time I wasted on it. I honestly didn't think it controlled me as much as it did (average 80-100 pickups a day and 6-8 hours use). I hang my head in guilt as my son used to regularly say to me, "Can you look at me Mum when I'm talking to you?" How bad is that??? I'm embarrassed to share that but it is a doozy of a reminder to lift one's head. Drastic action was required, an intervention!

Last year, on my birthday I decided to quit Social Media once and for all, or at least for a full year and then reassess. I had already ditched *Twitter* long ago, and for the previous couple of years I had only a couple of friends on *Facebook* as had unfollowed then removed everyone from that but kept the account and my business page, following similar businesses and pages of interest, as well as groups my son attended. So a final cutting of that thread didn't seem so bad. *Instagram* was going too, it was one of the worst for affecting my mood and depleting my energy.

In the time since stepping away for the sake of my health, which is what it came down to in the end, I have found that I missed it not a jot. I have been immensely happier, less anxious, less frustrated, less on-edge and less distracted. I no longer feel the need to share every political post that enrages me – I am not an oracle; it is not my responsibility to ensure everyone knows what's going on, it's up to each person to seek out the truth. We are all adults afterall. I don't take as many photos, don't share what photos I have taken and really don't want to share my life, I prefer to just live it. (Despite probably oversharing in this book...)

I have lived on line, publicly sharing, oversharing, cringing, having ah-ha moments, celebrations, arguments and more for thirteen years. With the fact that I needed to keep taking social media sabbaticals, I couldn't help but wonder (cue image of New York Brownstone building, upper window, woman gazing out the into the ether, pondering fingers poised above laptop keyboard): *has this been my lesson in this global pause – privacy?* The need to hold, protect and cherish that which I hold dear? And the answer was yes, I'm done with it, exhausted, spent. (If I'm being honest, this wasn't a great surprise to my system.) And in this digital age of global connectivity, I think, for me personally, leaving social media is quite possibly the wildest thing I could do!!! It reignited my inner rebel.

What if the wildest thing you could do was to reclaim, protect and honour your privacy?

Plus the freedom I gained when unplugged I now hold as precious.

What is surprising though when giving up social media and messenger, is that you lose friends, or rather acquaintances. People don't really text any more, it's all *Messenger* and *WhatsApp*. So if not using these services, then you quickly fall away. In addition to my chucking social media, my *iphone* decided to chuck me. It packed in, gave up the ghost wholesale in December of 2020 and has been replaced with an old 2g non-smart phone, which doesn't even have a camera on it. Purely text and talk and I love it. It's so cute and retro (made in 2011 doesn't yet qualify as vintage does it?). Whilst I have made many a friend/acquaintance via the web, this pandemic has reminded me that there are ways of connecting that don't involve a smart phone.

So, it was all was going fantastically well until I decided to write this book. No-one is going to know about it if I don't shout about it and the best way to do that? Social media!! Eight and a half months into my socials-free life I created a new *IG* account. I had already permanently deleted my *Facebook* business page with its thousand followers (I didn't know I would have a book to promote...) but I have absolutely zero intention of returning to that space, *IG* is enough, more than enough truth be told. I LOVE not being on social media. I am also thriving sans smart phone. While my wee purple flip phone is adorable, I rarely use it; texting is a nightmare and the only people who call are my mum and two close friends who also hate tech (Luddites unite!) and appreciate proper vocal conversation; a guid blether!

The call of a more analogue world is strong; ditching the digital is allowing the Wild to reawaken and arise. What's your relationship with social media and the influence digital tech has on your life and how does it impact upon your Sacred Soul Sustaining needs?

Simplifying my digital world hasn't been the only form of simplicity making its presence known in my world. I have also simplified my spiritual practice to just going with my internal calling and needs.

Heeding our intuition is a super power!

I love learning and seeking out new information to enhance and grow my own knowledge, but I don't like being *told* or *preached to,* preferring to feel into what I trust and what I accept. But more and more I feel so much of the knowledge and purported wisdom is heavy and laden with the 'right way' or cultural appropriation, which goes against my personal ethos. At this point in life, simplifying my lifestyle has me in a calmer state. I am happiest when out in the woods or walking the canal tow-path foraging, or at home kitchen-witchin and stitchin-witchin; I'm a crafter, a maker, a bringer together of the elements of the fabric of life. Coorying into my hearth is my sanctuary and my solitary practice is my true joy.

Other ways that I honour my SSS needs, which you might useful too, are :

- Tracking, tuning into and honouring my menstrual cycle in all her phases as previously discussed,
- Daily spiritual practice whether it is getting outside, meditation, working with the moon and seasons or using intuition in Tarot,
- Journalling is a must for me, morning pages or journaling my spiritual workings, making plans for coming week etc. Pencil, paper, and peace equals sacred bliss,
- Women's Circles are a biggie for just releasing what is inside, feeling heard and for being able to turn that gratitude into doing the same for others,
- Boundaries are a necessity. Finding out who will honour a boundary and who will take offence at the need for them is crucial,
- Eating well and paying attention to my body. Is it hungry or thirsty, is my skin dry, why the headache? Cutting out food that I have intolerances to has helped dramatically in both my mental and physical health and well being. Despite being delicious, macaroni cheese stops being sustenance when it causes me pain!
- Dance (barefoot and/or naked under the full moon if that's your fancy). Attending the ecstatic dance class I used to go to pre lock down was a full mind body and spirit exercise,
  Shake, Woman, shake.
  Dance, Woman, dance.
  Unleash. Rise. Express.
- Not peopling when I need to be on my own. Avoiding the torture of small talk and being upbeat and chatty when depleted is all part of taking care of

me. This is my ultimate SSS priority: **Solitude**. I NEED time on my own to recharge. No noise, no chatter, no drama, no tongue biting, no people, nothing. Whether that's being up early before the rest of the household to have my coffee or take a walk in the woods on my own, the need to be alone is absolute. To be fair, it's as much for me as for other people who come into contact with me...

While I am perfectly sure that we are all aware of how important it is to look after ourselves, I wonder how many of us actually take heed. There are numerous obstacles to taking the necessary care of ourselves other than the basics. Obstacles such as:

- Guilt. I suffer from this and it's guilt placed on our own shoulders from ourselves not necessarily from our children or partners or parents or careers (well, maybe your career, depending upon your boss...),
- Other people's opinions, our own opinions and inner critics,
- Lack of time,
- Lack of finances,
- Prioritising other "things" over SSS in deliberate self sabotage for any of the aforementioned obstacles,
- Prioritising the care of others over ourselves, particularly children, partners, other dependents, employers,
- The feeling of "I can do it all", "I'm managing fine" as proof of no need to pander to indulgences; being a martyr,
- Not believing we are worthy of what we perceive SSS to be,

- Exhaustion (if ever there was a reason to ensure you take time for yourself, here it is!)
- The social media vortex.

We need to address these barriers and obstacles, because if we don't how can we properly look after ourselves and meet all of our needs? If we are meeting everyone else's needs while sacrificing our own, what good is that to anyone? None, that's what! While we are all peace and love and (((hugs))) for our friends and family, how about we extend those feelings and words of wisdom to ourselves? We're worth it.

19

Rituals & Practices

Any ritual is an opportunity for transformation
~ Starhawk ~

Ritual; what imagery does that word conjure in your imagination? Sorcerers and auld witchy hags making sacrifices upon an altar? Or family traditions that happen round the festive period? Perhaps it moves your mind in a more structured fashion towards a mental or physical tick list of tasks or checks that must be done before leaving the house for example, or before going on holiday or leaving the office. Practice infers learning and repetition, right? Whether with religious connotations or habitual ones, these are rituals and practices in their own right.

Cambridge English Dictionary defines Ritual as:

- *A set of actions or words performed in a regular way, often as part of a religious ceremony*

- *A ritual is also any act done regularly, usually without thinking about it.*

The Free Dictionary defines Practice as:

- *To do or perform habitually or customarily; make a habit of*
- *To do or perform (something) repeatedly in order to acquire or polish a skill*
- *To carry out in action; observe: practices a religion piously.*

For me I would describe a ritual as an act of grounding or centering and is focused, sacred, and intentional. There is comfort and familiarity to be found in ritual and practice. A knowing of what's happening and why, it helps to reset and recalibrate one's self if knocked off course. Regular attendees to my Women's Circles will be familiar with the ritual and practices I have created for them, and feel both the benefits of and the joy they bring. Oh yes, I love rituals and have many. Some are sacred and others are probably more "routine" but ritual is far more pleasing a word to my sensibilities.

So what kinds of rituals or practices would I consider to be sacred? Let us start with the morning ritual. Do you have a morning routine? A ritual, a practice, a rhythm? A way to set yourself up for the day ahead? Or are you more of a fly by the seat of your breeks kinda gal?

Morning routines are very trendy right now. *YouTube* has umpteen videos demonstrating such. Perhaps you have a pattern you flow through daily but never thought to call it a "morning routine" because it's just life and has no need for a label.

I have a morning ritual, and it is sacred (and is so, because I said so). I need this time because it gives me time to think, to prepare myself mentally for the day ahead and just gives me some space. I am very much a morning person but absolutely NOT a morning *people* person. We live in a multi generational household with a lot of hormones and a distinct lack of inner monologues and filters, that the need for my ritual is a very deliberate act of Sacred Soul Sustenance.

Why do I refer to my morning tasks as a ritual rather than routine? Because it is a conscious and deliberate practice. It is carried out with intention and focus. I sometimes mix it up depending on how I'm feeling or whether my husband is at home or still at work (he works night shift). It is not done out of duty or on auto pilot or without careful consideration. I am not wish washy or half arsed during this time. Having a shower then brushing my teeth and getting dressed is routine. Prepping the coffee machine and organising my vitamins is routine. Getting down to the actuals of what forms my daily practice is ritual. This time is personal, private and unapologetically *mine*. My pattern is part ritual, part routine and together they form the rhythm of my morning. This is how the vast majority of my mornings go, but sometimes I have to adapt and sometimes I miss out everything altogether, but when I do, I feel a bit undone and on a back foot for the whole day. I miss the clarity and the breathing space of being on my own. As an introvert (yes an introvert, I'm an opinionated, effervescent introvert!) I need this to recharge, to be able to give the best of me to me, my family, to their needs and to live this life the best I can.

As we already know, all life is a cycle of phases, moving from one to next to the next. Mornings suit me perfectly just now, and I can't see that changing in the near future, but if and when the time comes that mornings don't work, my ritual will evolve to accommodate the new circumstance. Also the content of my ritual time has changed and evolved over time, adjusting to what it is I need and want from it.

Maybe a morning routine/ritual doesn't work with your current situation and the evening is more appropriate if your life is busy, possibly with raising children, or balancing two jobs, or work and college or caring for elderly relations, or in poor health yourself, physically or mentally. The effects of the past year of being in lock down, then not, then back again has left many routines and rhythms all topsy turvy and off kilter. We all have different circumstance and responsibilities that dictate what time we have to take to give to ourselves. But I will say, please try to carve out a space, reshuffle or reassess a priority or two in your schedule to ensure you have time that is just for you to do what you need to do to get some head space and clarity for what you want and how you can achieve it. I know you have goals and dreams, and you deserve to make them your reality, no matter how small or grand they may be. Even if it is just to sit down for 5 mins with a hot cuppa and a slice of cake.

Speaking of which; making that first cuppa of the day. Take that half-awake-on-auto-pilot state, light a candle and make the act of preparing your cuppa, or preferred beverage, a daily ritual. Deliberate and conscious rather than just going through the motions, the candle helps here rather than the big light, especially in the dark mornings. Take time to enjoy your drink, savour the flavour (and the aroma if it's coffee). Some folk may think this sounds a bit pretentious, but try it, it's not and creates a really gentle start to your day.

Journalling. Did you keep a diary as a teenager? My journalling love began when I was about 12 and received my first leather 5 year diary with a little clasp at the front. I wrote in it faithfully then about a year later, I went through it and *Tipexed* everything out. What if anyone read it? Over the years since, I have gone through periods where I have been very detailed in my entries and others, well, to describe my written experiences as "sparse" would be generous.

Do you keep a journal now? As an adult, journalling is a prominent feature in my life. It is both a practice and a ritual which forms part of my morning ritual time. I keep and have kept all sorts of journals and I find it easier to offload onto paper than out loud to another person. Once my thoughts are out, I can let them go. Once they are on the page I can begin to work through them like a puzzle to solve or an idea to develop and grow. It is an incredibly freeing and private way to collect myself. But sometimes a block can come up and the ideas dry up or something happens that causes a phase of second guessing myself or challenges a previous view. In these times I have found journal prompts to be helpful for jump starting my thoughts and getting me thinking and creating again. Journalling is a process which allows for calm, rest and reflection. Certainly in the past 6 years, daily journaling has been not only my ritual in ~~self care~~ Sacred Soul Sustenance but also my therapy.

Meditation. Creating and maintaining a meditation ritual takes practice but is so worth it.

Chanting "Ommm" whilst sitting legs crossed in lotus pose, thumbs and index fingers touching, eyes closed. That's meditation, right? Remaining in that position for half an hour or multiple hours, with an empty mind seeking inner peace? Well, no, that's not how my practice goes. Not at all in fact.

I use several different methods when meditating, depending upon the circumstances and where I am. For instance, if I need to calm down, take a time out or collect myself in a stressful situation, I focus on my breathing. This can be done anywhere at any time! No need for candles or incense to do this, the car or a public loo if needed are perfectly suitable. All I do is take a deep breath in through my nose, counting slowly as I do so. Hold the breath for the same amount of time plus 1 second, then slowly exhale the breath for the same length of time as inhale plus 2 seconds. It doesn't matter (to me) if I exhale through my nose or my mouth. This slows my heart rate and allows for clearer, calmer thinking and a better mood for continuing with my day or situation. This always works when I practice it, I just need to remember to practice it more...

Another method I use, if I need a more specific focus or advice, is much more recognisable as a form of "meditation" as it does involve sitting down in a comfortable position (the lotus pose doesn't work for me, I prefer a comfy chair if I am honest) and sometimes I do burn candles or incense, but I absolutely need time and peace and quiet on my own. In this practice I have a place, a home, I go to in my mind and can seek assistance or guidance from my circle of inspirational advisors, which is essentially a group of women (real and fictitious) who chip in with their tuppence worth during these sessions. Over the years my circle has changed with various members of my imaginary council being replaced, and their numbers have both increased and decreased as I have evolved. I started out with six women on my team which has grown to twelve, with me being the thirteenth. Never more than twelve, but sometimes only one. The only constant factor that has always been, is that my advisory squad has been made solely of women.

The other place I find it very easy to meditate, believe it or not, is in the shower! The motion of washing my hair is a no brainer requiring zero effort, which leaves plenty mind space to gather and process my thoughts. I often have my best ideas and moments of inspiration as I lather and rinse!

If you have never meditated before, it can seem a little daunting, or difficult with the unsure feeling of where to start or even knowing what the point of meditation is, if not for finding inner peace. There are lots of books on how to meditate and why, plus *YouTube* has a variety of videos to watch or listen to as a guided meditative practice. I would recommend even just starting with the breathing exercise I use. If you want to sit in lotus, or create a dedicated sacred space at home for your practice, do it. If you want to light candles or incense, do it. Or don't. There are no rules here, and the practice is entirely yours. It is worth noting though, that it is nigh on impossible to completely clear your mind, it will wander off in all directions, but as soon as you notice it going off on its own tangent, bring it back by refocussing on that breath. It takes, you guessed it, practice.

Candle meditation is another good one to start with as all it requires is gazing into the flame of a solitary candle (a pillar candle, votive or tea light, actually a birthday cake candle will do in an emergency!); nothing more. This is useful when needing to relax as your focus is on that flame, and your breath. Observe the flame as it dances, takes on different shapes and directions, whether it flickers or sways, notice if the colour changes. Start with 5 mins building it up over time to as long as you need or feel is necessary.

I keep referring to meditation as a practice because practice is what it takes. Practice to get comfortable with what you are doing, with what you want to achieve and practice to make it a regular part of your routine, rhythm or ritual. I have been "practising" for the past 19 years but have yet to establish a proper and regular habit. It's very much ad hoc and fitting it in when I either remember or feel the need, or incorporate it into a specific ritual.

Personal rituals such as living in sync with your own personal rhythm of your menstrual cycle; charting it to learn and become familiar with where you are in your cycle and how you are likely to feel on certain days, spread throughout the year and during each of the months in turn is a very grounding, beautiful and stabilising practice. (See how menstrual cycle tracking keeps coming up?)

New and Full Moon rituals each month and/or the changing seasons, using the **Wheel of the Year**, help us to align with what is happening in nature and within ourselves as discussed in Thread 2.

New Years Resolutions or selecting a **Word of the Year** are also rituals that require thought, deliberation and intention as they are thought out and worked through.

Affirmations. A great many people love affirmations and find them useful and inspiring. Using them is a practice of repetition and belief, reaffirming the affirmation. Often affirmations are used each morning, looking in the mirror and reciting your affirmation to your self, such as *I am loved* or *I am worthy, I am healthy* etc. Personally, I have not found them to work for me, I don't feel comfortable or authentic reciting them, but I do have a couple of little ones in my planner that I look at every now and again, just as a wee reminder. The late Louise L. Hay has a phenomenal collection of affirmations, and I incorporate written affirmations which have been greatly welcomed, in Circle.

Women's Circles. Not all practices or rituals are solo efforts. A Women's Circle where the purpose is to bring us together, to support and encourage and share. A practice which is incredibly uplifting and sacred. The ritual, meditation and connection is deeply felt and revered.

Switching Off. In these modern times of fast living and instant information and connection, it takes and is a true practice to purposely switch off, be that our monkey brain or our devices. When we switch off the white noise and bustle to slow down, we reconnect with our senses. We notice more, feel more and appreciate more.

Switching off allows for plugging back into real life with real people in real time.

Time out. We've heard about disciplining kids by putting them in a time out, an enforced period of time without their toy of choice or just some time alone to breathe, but what about if we flip the time out into a valuable practice instead? Make a dedicated effort to put ourselves in a time out. What would that look like?

The Sacred Practice of Pausing :

- A Pyjama Day. In the pre Covid lock down world this may be a step too far for some people, but the thought of a pyjama day certainly had its appeal. Throughout my working life I have thrown the odd sickie for this very purpose. In hindsight I was really just looking after myself to recharge before going back to work the very next day. Not convinced my employers would have agreed though.
- Uninterrupted Bubble Bath. The time in the tub can range from 15 mins to over an hour; that time is sacred and sublime. Create yourself a special bathing ritual with specific oils or salts just for this time.
- Reading. In my opinion, pressing pause on life for a moment to escape and breathe can rarely be found anywhere else other than between the pages of a good book, but then I am a book worm. Magazines,

brochures, comics, graphic novels, newspapers and blog posts, are perfect to pick up and dive into to have a little time out - be it on the commute to work if using public transport, in bed before going to sleep instead of scrolling Facebook or Instagram, with a cuppa on the couch or in the park while your children play. Dedicating time to read a chapter is a practice in itself, especially if you are not a regular reader for pleasure.

- Music is another beauty that presses all the pause buttons, whether you are listening to or playing (practising) an instrument. Getting lost in the music as it surrounds you. Music is extremely evocative. Let go and dance or sing and join in, in which ever way the music calls to you.
- Dancing. Whether in a class or in your kitchen it doesn't matter, just dance with wild abandon, without ego, to release, to surrender, for freedom, for you!
- No. The practice of pause can often mean saying NO and meaning it. When you say yes to all the stuff you are surrounded with day in day out and people are depending on you, it can be tough to say no. But saying NO, you must. The world will not collapse because you are finishing the chapter of your book or sitting in meditation or doing something that honours you and your needs.
- Art or craft. Remember when you were a kid and the simple joy that colouring in brought? Or the satisfaction from crafting "something"? Painting, writing, scrap-booking, cooking, baking, sewing, knitting, pyrography, pressing flowers, drying herbs, you get the idea. Making lends itself easily to creating rituals around your practice, be it around collecting your materials, the preparation for beginning, the

actual process of creating itself. There are no limits here.
- Wild swimming. This is a practice that is gaining popularity particularly with women. Swimming in the freezing waters is reported to be an exhilarating experience, fantastic for the circulation, life affirming, and every possible positive adjective under the sun. I have to 'fess up and state that this is one activity that is categorically not for me. I prefer to live vicariously through other people's *insta* photos when it comes to getting in a loch in -3 degrees or swimming in the north sea at sunrise. Even with the promise of a hot cuppa post swim and a roaring campfire on the beach. I fear that the cold would do irreparable damage to my already granny-status bladder and I cannot handle the pain from frozen nipples. Even in a wet suit and a woolly hat. It does look wonderful though, so crack on and post your pics for me to enjoy!

If looking at the list and thinking "ahh, that would be nice" or "chance would be a fine thing", I'm here to tell you that, yes, it is nice and it is indeed a fine thing, when the opportunity to do so is created or diarised and prioritised. I'm also here to tell you (again) that if you don't make your own sacred practices and rituals important, no-one else will. You don't need anyone's permission. If, however, you still feel like you do need permission then I am giving you that permission. There, done!

You are sacred, you are worthy, you are invaluable, you are sovereign and you are whole. You are someone who deserves to be respected and treated as such, first and foremost by yourself!

Awaken Your Wild You

20

Remember Reconnect Reclaim

Meditation

Waters of Truth

Sitting or lying down comfortably, close your eyes. Inhale deeply through your nose, filling your lungs and your heart space. Exhale slowly. Inhale again, expanding your core down to your womb space. Exhale slowly. Inhale slowly and deeply filling your entire being. Exhale fully from your mouth, every last particle of air.

Take a moment here to just breathe. Starting with the top of your head, visualise scanning your way down your entire body, sensing if there are any niggles, tightness or discomfort. Pause where you find tension and breathe into the spot for 2 breaths before slowly moving on all the way down to your toes. How do you feel now?

You are on a journey to awaken your wild you. Focus your

attention on your heart centre; how does it feel? What is it telling you about who your inner Wild is? (pause for a breath) Shift your focus down to your womb space. How does it feel? What is it telling you about your inner Wild's desires and passions? (pause for a breath) Move your attention up to your mind. How does that feel? What is it telling you about your inner Wild's priorities and focus? (pause for a breath)

Imagine now that you are standing in the mouth of a cave. You can hear what sounds like a waterfall deep within. It sounds melodic and you are drawn to its tune. You walk deeper into the cave and notice the music gets louder as though it is calling you forth. Follow the sound.

You reach the waterfall. It is indeed playing the most beautiful tune you've ever heard. This music is just for you. How do you feel? (pause for a breath)

The water cascades down into a pool of the clearest crystal water. What else do you notice about this place? How is it lit? How does it smell? Is it warm or cool? Take it all in. (pause for two breaths)

You step down to the water's edge and have an urge to dive in, or at least paddle in the shallows. There is no-one else here, just you. You are alone and you are completely safe. This is your time. You begin to undress, leaving your clothes discarded on the rock by your side. As you shed your material layers, you realise you are shedding other layers too; the shoulds of life, imposed upon you by yourself, by family, friends and society. You are casting off dramas you've been dawn into, peeling away labels you've been assigned. Off and off they all fall. The more you remove, the more you can breathe and the lighter you feel. Toss aside past regrets, mistakes and negative self talk. Strip away the longing and confusion as to who you think you ought to be. None of these layers define you. Let all of that go with the last garment of clothing. How do you feel now, standing there naked by the pool? Unburdened? Free? Vulnerable? (pause for as long as you need)

Step into the water. It is warm on your skin like a luxurious bath. You walk into the pool as far as you feel comfortable. Feel the waters wash away the residual layers, those deep ingrained opinions and thoughts of who you have been told you are and of the life you are living. As you float, swim or paddle you are calm and have a sense of complete peace. Breathe in that peace. You are you, pure you in the here and now. Enjoy the feeling. Allow it to flow through your body as the water holds you. (pause for as long as you need)

Listen to the melody of the waterfall. This is your theme tune; your song which plays only for you. As you focus on the power of the music, the curtain of water thins and you can see through it. There is somewhere beyond this place. You walk or swim over to and through the waterfall and feel its soft waters cleanse you. On the other side of the waterfall you find yourself in a beautiful, warm chamber, the walls are made of quartz. There is another pool in the centre, a much smaller pool, whose water is so still it looks like glass.

You gaze into the pool and see your reflection staring back out at you. Your reflection is showing you what you need to see; is it your real true you? Is it revealing where you need to focus your sacred soul sustenance? Is it your heart's desire? Who is your Wild? You are a soul of being, of intention, of purpose, of truth, of worth. What do you see? (pause for as long as you need)

Take in all you see and feel. Absorb it all. As you continue to gaze into the reflection, be open to any messages you receive. (pause)

You are ready to leave the chamber but there is only one way out; through a doorway at the rear that you hadn't noticed. There is a clothes rail next to the door. Your discarded clothes that you shed on the other side of the waterfall are hung up on the rail. You need to redress before leaving. You look at the garments available and see those same clothes hanging alongside different and new pieces. You can choose what you want to dress in. Do any of your old layers still fit? Are they a comfy fit? Or will you pick something new but true and wild? (pause for a breath)

Once redressed in fabric and your values, and with the inner wisdom of knowing how to nurture and nourish your needs, you leave the cave. The cave will always be here to welcome you, to swim and bathe in its waters, to show you your true reflection, because this cave is within you.

Take a satisfying deep breath in and release. Feel the light expanse of your chest as your breathe in again, and slowly release. On your next breath begin to wiggle your toes and fingers and, when you are ready, open your eyes.

Welcome back.

Journal Prompts

- Am I playing small with my dreams and passion or am I writing my best story?

- Where to I go and what do I do to recharge my batteries? To reconnect to myself, to refresh, refuel, remember, release, reflect and rewild?
- What are my habits and practices? Do I consider them to be rituals?
- Do I choose a Word of the Year? Or do I prefer resolutions? Or both? How do I decide?
- Is there anything I would like to start doing or need to stop doing?
- Do I consider my needs to be a priority? Or do I play the martyr? Why?
- Is self care, or Sacred Soul Sustenance, a regular practice for me or is it way down on my to-do list?
- How do my values align with my SSS practice?
- Is there anything in my everyday life that I could simplify?
- When was the last time I switched off my devices and took a break from social media?
- How do I feel about a possible week or month away from social media?
- What obstacles are currently preventing me from maintaining my Sacred Soul Sustenance?

Actions

- Find out and explore what it is that lights you up from with in.
- Schedule time in your diary or pop it on the calendar, specific time for yourself to engage in a practice or ritual for your own needs.
- Create a specific ritual and dedicate yourself and your time to carrying it out. Don't make it complicated or it will be harder to keep to.

- Try different meditation styles and see what works for you and commit to cultivating a regular practice.
- Take a social media break and switch off. What do you do with that free time? Notice how you feel when disconnected to the internet.

*Mirror Mirror,
on the wall,
Am I pretty?
Am I small?
My mind is walking
through the maze,
Figuring out best
what pleases society's gaze.
Am I quiet?
Am I polite?
Am I conforming
To patriarchal shite?
I am beautiful.
I am bold.
I define my own standards,
I'm done with being told.
I am unique.
I am me.
I'm over this bullshit.
I am free!*

~ Lissa Corra ~

Conclusion

She is awake.
She is free. Her heart is expansive and once again she feels the air in her lungs, the fire of creation alight in her womb. She hears her voice speaking her truth, her body is taking up space, her space, her rightful place. She is connected to you, to herself, to the Great Mother, to the past, the present and the tomorrow yet to be, as she gently reminds you:

"I am you, you are me, we are SHE."

You've made it! Thank you for staying the course and reaching this point. How are you feeling? Are you ready to go round again? This journey is never ending. It, like everything else in these pages, is cyclic, we just have more experience that we did that last round and the one before. There is no final destination in the awakening as we are constantly learning, living, adapting, growing, evolving, transforming, experiencing, unlearning, changing our minds, resetting and adjusting as we feel called to do.

I hope that while your experiences are different to mine, you were able to identify with the themes and were able to reflect upon your own experience, values and points of view from perhaps a new angle.

The recurring themes that came through were the cyclic nature of life and how all life is connected yet at the same time all life and experiences and interpretations of said life are unique. It's about finding what works and is true for you as the sovereign woman you are.

> ***I am me.***
> ***I am who I'm meant to be.***
> ***I am my past, my present***
> ***and who I want to be.***
> ***I am not any one,***
> ***I am all three,***
> ***a work in progress, a destiny.***
> ***I am me.***

I hope too that you have been able to (re)discover the simple joys that led you to this path in the first place. A new or revitalised love and reverence for what is important to you and how you go about honouring that and yourself, breathing deeply without any niggles or discomfort. Seeking acceptance, acknowledgement and approval from external sources is over, done, the need is unhealthy and unnecessary. Knowing that everything you seek is all within. Of course learn the wisdoms and knowledge from books or people you respect or just from life itself, but the validation or the guidance for what is right for you comes from *you*. While we have all picked up habits along the way over the years that were not beneficial to us for whatever reason, I believe that they had to be experienced to fully appreciate them and to be able to understand why they weren't right as part of the continuous cycle of life that we are living; waxing and waning, receiving and relieving, letting go. They were all just phases of varying length. A cycle.

If you take nothing else away with you from this book, please remember there is no right way, wrong way or only way, just *your* way. Whether your inner Wild is fast asleep, beginning to awaken or is wide awake, caffeinated and good to go, She is you and no-one can take her away from you.

Sovereignty
Truth
Wisdom

Lissa Corra

Acknowledgements

First and foremost I would like to take this opportunity to thank Steve, Archie and Helen for living through this process with me; I know it hasn't been easy, but we did it! You've all had to pick up the slack at home and while I felt guilty about about that at the time, this book would never have been finished without you doing your own damn dishes ;) And specifically to my husband, Steve, for always supporting and believing in my writing and creative endeavours, be they half arsed or fruitful and for keeping my spirits up when they start to flail. I love you.

My deepest gratitude to Leigh Barnard, Anna Wren Kelly, Rosey Crow, Holly Elissa, Carolyn Stewart and my Mum for reading through my drafts and giving me their thoughts and feedback on the book at the different stages. Your comments kept me going to finish the book. Sorry Mum, the Fbombs stayed!

Thank you to Florence Pritchard (my Mum), June Dormer, Helen Orr, Nancy McKendry, Jayne Galloway, Maria Hunter, Nicola Tams, Gemma Tierney, Jen Douglas, Lesley Gardiner and Fiona Morrison for responding to my S.O.S. on the topic of the Crone and offering up their wisdoms on ageing. I am grateful for your honesty and truth.

And finally, to Aphra Wilson, without you there would no book here right now, thank you for wanting to publish my words and providing the opportunity to make a long held dream come true.

About the Author

Lissa Corra
Mother, Ceremonial Priestess and Writer.

Lissa is the daughter of Florence, granddaughter of Margaret, great-granddaughter of Susan, great-great-granddaughter of Elizabeth, great-great-great-granddaughter of Margaret. She is also a mum and wife.

Through the power of Circle, she gathers the women around her hearth fire in sacred space sharing the wisdoms and celebrating their stories, honouring their needs, weaving the connecting threads of sisterhood. She encourages women to recognise, reclaim and rejoice in their rites of passage, connection to the earth and to the ancestors.

She is also something of a coffee snob and adores fresh brewed coffee, not instant. Period dramas are her favourite TV (with a soft spot for Hercule Poirot). She reads cookery book like novels, is passionate about politics and the environment, has a love/hate relationship with social media and doesn't have a smart phone. Pottering around in her garden brings her joy as does sitting out in the evening with a small fire burning and her family by her side.

Awaken Your Wild You

Printed in Great Britain
by Amazon